m2uk
33

SHAKESPEARE DANCING

Shakespeare Dancing

A Theatrical Study of the Plays

John Russell Brown

First published 2005 by
PALGRAVE MACMILLAN
Houndmills, Basingstoke, Hampshire RG21 6XS and
175 Fifth Avenue, New York, N.Y. 10010
Companies and representatives throughout the world

PALGRAVE MACMILLAN is the global academic imprint of the Palgrave
Macmillan division of St. Martin's Press, LLC and of Palgrave Macmillan Ltd.
Macmillan® is a registered trademark in the United States, United Kingdom
and other countries. Palgrave is a registered trademark in the European
Union and other countries.

ISBN 1–4039–4195–5 hardback
ISBN 1–4039–4196–3 paperback

This book is printed on paper suitable for recycling and made from fully
managed and sustained forest sources.

A catalogue record for this book is available from the Library of Congress.

10   9   8   7   6   5   4   3   2   1
14 13 12 11 10 09 08 07 06 05

Printed in China

Contents

Preface

When I first planned this book I was not sure I would be understood or whether other writers shared the same mind. I would be writing from the belief that Shakespeare's imagination was physical as well as verbal, that sensation was his primary inspiration, and that he used words not for their own sake but to give rise to many and various performances for audiences in theatres. This conviction has been growing for some time but I have not previously set out to show how it influences the way I read the plays and try to stage them. Previously I have assumed, as I think almost everyone does, that we must try to understand the words of a text and imagine them being spoken as part of a performance. Now I want to put sensation before everything else – laughter, fear, excitement, jealousy, love, affection, peace and the very presence of actors – rather than giving sole attention to intellectual thought or argument. The words of a text are vital elements in the performance of Shakespeare's plays and without them there would be no performance, but words are not alone definitive and certainly not unchanging in effect. The dance of theatre that I want to write about is the imaginary origin of these plays, the seed from which they sprung. Physical enactment in time and space, and not the speaking of their texts, is the element for which Shakespeare wrote and in which his plays were to live.

This is a practical book. A number of specific examples lead towards a wider view of the nature of the plays and the rewards they offer. The last chapter calls for an experiential criticism: one that is attentive to sensation, as well as to theme or argument, and, in reference, is both personal and social. Almost all the material is taken from well-known plays so that readers will be able to contribute a fuller context from their own knowledge of the texts and experience of the plays in performance. Each chapter concludes with a summary of its practical applications.

I have been greatly indebted to the actors and students with whom I have worked in recent years, especially those of New Fortune Theatre and the graduate course in Directing at Middlesex University: I could not have written this book without their help. I have special debts to John Faulkner, the Producer for the theatre company and my generous counsellor and supporter; to Girish Karnad, Director of the Nehru Centre in London, and Michael Freeman of the Bloomsbury UCL Theatre, both of whom have provided facilities for rehearsal and performance; and to Leon Rubin and other colleagues at Middlesex who have befriended and contributed to my research. I am particularly indebted to the criticism of trusted colleagues and friends who read a first draft of this book: Tony Thorlby, Robert Shaughnessy, Bridget Escolme, and Randall Martin. I have tried to make good use of their comments and the book is much the better for them. A few chapters draw upon articles already published elsewhere. I am grateful for permission to reproduce and develop these earlier accounts, as acknowledged in notes at appropriate places. Unless otherwise noted, all references to Shakespeare's plays are from Peter Alexander's edition (London: Collins, 1951), which is kept constantly in print.

While the book was taking shape and nearing completion it had the benefit of sensitive and generous guidance from Anna Sandeman, its commissioning editor at Palgrave Macmillan. As it progressed towards publication Kate Wallis, with Sonya Barker, took over her responsibilities and my copy-editors, Valery Rose and Jocelyn Stockley, were marvellously helpful and enlightening. Turning my typescript into a book, at all stages, was a pleasure and added much to its realization. I am most grateful.

28 April 2004   J. R. B.

Introduction

For Orpheus' lute was strung with poets' sinews,
Whose golden touch could soften steel and stones,
Make tigers tame, and huge leviathans
Forsake unsounded deeps to dance on sands.
                    (*The Two Gentlemen of Verona*, III.ii.78–81)

Written early in Shakespeare's career, these words were
prophetic. The changing dynamic of his plays drew audiences to performances that could be as sensational as the
dancing of leviathans. When a play ends, both actors and
audience can be left wondering what has happened, so
far have they been transported.

Everywhere in Shakespeare's plays words awaken sensuous images and call for embodiment. In his imagination,
he must have seen and felt the physical consequences of
thought: a lute is *strung* and, in an image both tangible
and fantastic, a musician's *touch* is *golden*. In the mind,
steel, *stones*, *tigers*, and *sand* can all be palpable, oceans *unsounded*, and poets implicated by their very *sinews*. For a
reader, as for actors and audience, a play-text provides a
stream of sensuous provocation that sets imagination to
work and awakens memories of lived experience. Any of
the senses may be called upon, hearing and touch as well
as sight, and even the taste of freshness or decay. Every literary artifice is put to work in this way: simile, metaphor,
imagery, choice of words, metre, rhythm, syntax, and
more. Allusions and double meanings suggest different
levels of consciousness, creating a subtext of feelings and
sensations that underlie speech. In rehearsal or performance, or with careful and repeated reading of the text,

1

further palpable images register and mingle with earlier ones. This appeal to the senses and suggestion of physical activity are distinctive qualities of Shakespeare's writing. His imagination brought an entire world into lively play, as if dancing on the shifting sands that border the mind's ocean.

* * *

Shakespeare's plays would be very much easier to study if they were not so sensational, if they did not constantly ask readers and playgoers to respond with their senses as well as their verbalizing intelligence. Hamlet's most famous soliloquy starts with abstract thought plainly expressed, but, after one line, it passes on to speak of a mind that suffers as if from specific acts of physical aggression:

> To be, or not to be – that is the question;
> Whether 'tis nobler in the mind to *suffer*
> The *slings* and *arrows* of outrageous fortune, ...

It continues to speak of taking action against fortune's onslaught, as if Hamlet were struggling with an imaginary and restless sea:

> Or to take arms against a sea of troubles,
> And by opposing end them.

From now on, references multiply to off-stage events that in performance can so quicken an actor's imagination that Hamlet seems to participate in them and communicate to an audience the accompanying sensations: what it feels like to *die, sleep, dream, wish, shuffle off, give pause*, to experience *heart-ache* and *shock*, and to be frustrated by an unforeseen *rub*. Events from real-life are recalled:

> ... the whips and scorns of time,
> Th' oppressor's wrong, the proud man's contumely,

The pangs of despis'd love, the law's delay,
The insolence of office, …

(*Hamlet,* III.i.56ff.)

In performance, the soliloquy achieves far more than a verbal expression of conscious thought. If an actor's imagination is committed to even a few of the images, his speech will awaken such physical reactions in himself that an audience will *see* what is happening to the man, besides *hearing* what he says. In their imaginations spectators can come to share Hamlet's sensations and seem to live in his time and place.

In *Much Ado About Nothing,* Beatrice has a soliloquy in a very different vein, less dense with images and yet sharply felt. Tricked into believing that Benedick is 'well-nigh dead' with unrequited love for her (V.iv.81), she speaks of her feelings as if they were physical sensations. At the start, she recognizes a 'fire' in her ears, and her quick-moving thoughts draw to a close in the resolve to tame her 'wild heart'. In her imagination, the feelings she experiences are like an unfettered beast needing to be governed by a 'loving hand' (III.i.107–16). Then she thinks of their loves 'bound up' in the holy 'band' of matrimony and momentarily believes that her behaviour will conform to the new situation. While others have said that Benedick is well-deserving, she now believes it 'better than reportingly' (ll. 115–16); she has actually experienced its truth as fire and longed for the touch of his hand. If the actor has experienced these sensations in imagination so that they influence performance, an audience will see what is happening to the very being of Beatrice and share in her predicament.

Shakespeare has imagined the leading persons of his plays as complete human beings, not as voices only; for him, as he was writing, they were alive in body as well as mind. Words that express their conscious and, sometimes, unconscious thoughts will frequently also imply accompanying physical and sensuous impulses. In *Othello,* for example, when two troops of armed men confront each other, a single sentence does more than

give an order and demonstrate resilient command:
'Put up your bright swords, for the dew will rust them'
(I.ii.59). Shakespeare has imagined Othello seeing
swords drawn from their scabbards in the early morning
and immediately thinking that they could lose their
shine. In this moment of confrontation, as the general
mocks those surrounding him and unnecessarily preparing to fight, physical images of shining perfection and
its subsequent loss lie so deeply and surely within his
mind that they surface into words in this composed
form without hesitation. Attention will be concentrated
on Othello because, on this first entrance, he is standing
at the still centre of an active and excited crowd: an audience may sense his fear of corruption in a physical
tension or momentary swiftness, in the actor's posture,
set of mouth, or in the eyes. Physical command, sensuous response, and inward unease are all present as well
as speech.

Shakespeare set his plays in action on a stage and also
in an imagined world that was more extensive, varied,
strange and intimate than any ordinary reality, a context
in which thoughts can transform physical presence,
speech can become music and action a dance. The
persons of these plays exist somewhere between solid
reality and insubstantial illusion. On the one hand, performance necessarily involves the minds and bodies of
actors who live in the same time and place as their audience, speak words taken from everyday life, and carry out
the actions of ordinary events. And simultaneously, by ac-
tivating the imaginations of actors and audiences, the
plays awaken fantasies and transform memories so that
performance can both merge with and surpass what is
known of the real world. This volatile amalgam is experienced according to individual sensibilities, and varies in
immediacy and force during the course of a play's action.

As students who want to understand a text's theatrical
life, our search should keep moving between these two
polar opposites, between a recognizable and tangible
reality and a vivid, sensuous and perpetually changing illusion that sets our imaginations working. Considering

the meaning of words is only the necessary preliminary to becoming aware of what a play offers in performance.

* * *

In the texts, actors find many instructions to enact physically and many suggestions to awaken their imaginations and personal memories. A whole series of choices is involved to which each actor will respond differently in a process that is not always conscious and with effects that are not always controllable. Minor decisions and accidental changes can have a disproportionate influence on what a play becomes. Even the most ordinary words will alter in force, and sometimes in meaning, when they are spoken quickly or slowly, loudly or softly, lightly or emphatically. The many ways of saying 'No' or 'Yes' are everyday examples of how the impulse for speech will influence the sound of words and the messages they convey. How one line of Shakespeare's text is spoken can be no less variable. For example, delivery of each phrase can vary in 'Put up ... your bright swords ... or ... the dew ... will ... rust them.' And so it is with actions required by the text. Taking another person by the hand, moving closer or further apart, putting on clothes or taking them off, walking, sitting, kissing, fighting, or killing can all be performed in many ways, at different speeds, in silence, or when there is much else to compete for attention. The very presence of actors on stage can vary in confidence and energy: they can be responsive to others or out of sympathy, physically strong or nervously quick. All these elements of performance are so variable that what happens on stage is often affected by accident or thoughtless impulse. The effect of a single moment in a play, even in the same production, will never be the same from one day to another.

No performance of a Shakespeare play will be a 'true' or 'complete' rendering of the text. With a director in charge many details can be ordered according to one person's perception of the play but that control cannot be complete or give authority and permanence to any performance. Nor do any two members of an audience witness a production in the same way since they bring different expectations and predilections with them to the theatre; even when they notice the same features, they may do so in different ways and with different consequences. For all these reasons, the study of a play in performance has to take aim at a moving and ever changing target, the evidence for which varies greatly in importance and relevance.

These difficulties are not entirely avoided by turning one's back on theatre and studying Shakespeare's plays as any other printed books that reproduce, more or less accurately, the words set down by an author. Like it or not, any thoughtful attempt to make consecutive sense of all the words will carry the mind into the midst of action as well as speech. A sudden gap in what is being said, a change in direction of address, or an unexplained shift in topic, vocabulary, imagery, or tone will leave an attentive reader instinctively wanting to know more and allowing imagination to supply the action that is missing. If we open our minds to the dialogue as we are reading, we are bound to become entangled in uncertainties very similar to those of theatrical performance. We cannot see how each person looks or what exactly every one is doing, as we can in a theatre, but the text tells us that they move and breathe, and, as we read and the story unfolds, we begin to see what is happening in the mind's eye. We are led to imagine some of the sensations that lie behind the words in a speaker's mind and, soon, we seem to catch glimpses of action and hear snatches of speech. Shakespeare has written in such a way that a reader begins to respond to the words as if they were part of an imaginary, three-dimensional, and tangible existence, similar to that of theatrical performance and just as changeable and lacking in textual authority.

We are all drawn to bring our individual selves to seeing or reading these plays, our own past experiences of life and of art, our own ways of responding to what confronts us. In consequence, the experience is special to each person and no two will ever 'see' the same play, neither wanting nor being able to react in the same way. This is a natural process. In his *L'Imaginaire* (1966), Jean Paul Sartre distinguished three modes of perception by which we give 'psychological presence' to any phenomenon: we can *see* a house, *think* of a house, or *imagine* a house. While the first two of these functions are similar for most people, what the imagination perceives will differ widely. All three processes will be involved in creating and responding to works of art but imagination tends to be especially prominent when writing, acting, or witnessing a play. The closed environment of a theatre encourages imagination to be free so that it extends its reach and holds on to impressions. From a host of recorded testimonies, Hans van Maanen has demonstrated that a theatre audience, very frequently, recognizes that imagination is its dominant mode of perception.[1] Spectators soon begin to take over the performance so that what is presented on stage is re-created differently in their own minds, each one in a personal and unique way. Rather than *communicating* an author's vision or meaning to an audience, theatre is a site for *collaboration* between author, actors, and audience, all sharing in the creation of unprecedented imaginative experiences, a process that is also both intimate and individual.

Shakespeare's writing positively encourages imaginative response, and sometimes a text would make little or no consecutive sense without doing so. A scene that is crowded with people and driven forward by several different motivations can be hard to follow, even in performance, if imagination is not at hand. The riot that Iago engineers in Act II, scene iii, of *Othello* is an example of this:

OTHELLO   What is the matter here?
MONTANO   'Zounds, I bleed still; I am hurt to the death.
OTHELLO   Hold, for your lives!
IAGO   Hold, ho! Lieutenant – sir – Montano –
gentlemen –

Have you forgot all sense of place and duty?
Hold! The General speaks to you; hold, hold, for
                                                    shame!
OTHELLO   Why, how now, ho! From whence ariseth
                                                    this?
Are we turn'd Turks, and to ourselves do that
Which Heaven hath forbid the Ottomites?
For Christian shame, put by this barbarous brawl.
He that stirs next to carve for his own rage
Holds his soul light: he dies upon his motion.
Silence that dreadful bell; it frights the isle
From her propriety. What's the matter, masters?
Honest Iago, that looks dead with grieving,
Speak. Who began this? On thy love, I charge thee.
IAGO   I do not know... .

                                        (II.iii.156–70)

A reader must be alert to prevent the action becoming a confused blur in the mind. For members of an audience, the rapid changes of focus that the dialogue requires will set them looking at a number of simultaneous actions and cause much that is said and done to pass them by. Both reader and spectator are left to make what sense their imaginations can supply.

In these fifteen lines, the meaning of the words give a reader little reason to pause; the only passage not readily understood is Othello's allusion to the religious prohibition of fighting that was respected amongst the Ottomites. Why should an Islamic convert to Christianity refer to this issue during a public crisis and in this quibbling manner? While a reader is free to pass quickly over the two lines, an actor who has to make them credible in performance will need to project himself imaginatively into Othello's mind and being. Has this Moor become tense with instinctive self-awareness, either through pride or in anger? Or is he being deliberate and thoughtful, perhaps speaking with bitter irony? Or might his words be rash, spoken without a second thought? 'We' and 'ourselves' could imply that he associates himself with those who are disturbing the peace, or he might use these words in irony or reproof.

Consciously or unconsciously, from amongst many possibilities, an actor inevitably makes choices in order to
express the sensations and changing consciousness that
carry Othello through this crisis. He will then face other
decisions, since Othello now speaks of Christian morality
and, after that, dissociates himself from his listeners by
using pronouns in the third person. Prompted by the text
but without further guidance, an actor will have to
imagine all these shifts of awareness in order to present
Othello as a person who is convincingly and consecutively
alive in body and mind.

For an audience, words guide understanding but are
not responsible for all that is happening. Each spectator
will respond to different elements that go beyond what
speech communicates, and in imagination piece out what
performance offers. Individual and first-hand experience
of crowds and violent brawling, of drunkenness, military
discipline, religious practices and inhibitions, of personal
courage and fear, and much else – memories that are
unique to each reader, actor, and spectator – will be
drawn into reception of the play. By these means, hard to
explicate and never constant, the text is given a renewed
and substantial life on stage that can be readily accepted
as if it were actually happening and is uniquely re-created
on every occasion.

* * *

*Language was Shakespeare's instrument and without his words
the plays would not have survived to be performed today, but we
must look beyond words and around them in order to understand how he used them. Each chapter of this book examines one
element of what constitutes a theatrical event, and looks at
Shakespeare's handling of it in a number of texts. Some chapters
lead into each other, building up a composite view of a play or
relating one theatrical skill to another. Some deal with a few
short incidents in several plays so that certain aspects of
Shakespeare's art can be more fully explored than would be possible if only one or two plays were being studied. While acting is at*

or near the centre of every chapter, attention is also paid to other elements of production, such as visual effects, sound, music, and stage-management.

Some themes appear repeatedly throughout the book. What is imagination and how can we best understand its operation? How do plays that were written for audiences four hundred years ago work in performance today for a diverse public living in very different social, cultural, and political environments? In what respects are contemporary ways of producing, staging, and acting the plays adapted to the nature of Shakespeare's writing? How best can going to the theatre inform our study, and the other way around? The first chapter, which focuses on a number of comedies, deals with two issues scarcely hinted at yet: the role an audience can play in a performance and the use to be made of historical and literary research in theatrical study.

Note

1.   See Hans van Maanen, 'Perception', in *Theatrical Events: Borders, Dynamics, Frames,* ed. Vicky Ann Cremona et al. (Amsterdam: Rodopi, 2004). The reference here to Sartre's *L'Imaginaire: Psychologie phénoménologique de l'imagination* (1966) has been taken from this article, which also gives an exceptionally clear account of all aspects of a theatrical event. See, especially, the figures on pp. 244–5, 251, 253–4 and 259.

1
Present Laughter: Comedy in Performance

Comedies depend on their audiences, even more than other plays, because laughter is an unreliable and problematic phenomenon. It can be an almost mindless reflex but, at other times, a thoughtful, surprising, dangerous or hesitant response. We can laugh for very personal reasons when no one else does, or laugh along with everyone present. We can laugh *at* the persons on stage or *with* them, enjoying their company. Much will depend on our mood at the moment. As Rosaline tells Berowne in *Love's Labour's Lost*:

> A jest's prosperity lies in the ear
> Of him that hears it, never in the tongue
> Of him that makes it.
>
> (V.ii.849–51)

Text and actor are vital ingredients of a comedy but its life in performance and any meaning it communicates will also depend on its audience and how it responds. Study should take members of an audience into account, their day-to-day lives and interests, and their mood at the time and place of each performance.

* * *

11

A comedy is more than a collection of jests at the mercy of their audience but even a single burst of laughter can modify the effect of a whole play. Shakespeare some-times placed outright jokes – that have to raise laughter if they are not to fall flat and be tiresome – in positions where the principal persons of a play would otherwise hold close attention, their futures in the balance or awaiting fulfilment. In the last scene of *As You Like It*, Touchstone's account of the seven reasons for a quarrel and the seven degrees of a lie is a prime example of a 'jest's prosperity' transforming an audience's mood and its reception of much else. He enumerates the various degrees of a lie:

> The first, the Retort Courteous; the second, the Quip Modest; the third, the Reply Churlish; the fourth, the Reproof Valiant; the fifth, the Countercheck Quarrelsome; the sixth, the Lie with Circumstance; the seventh, the Lie Direct.
>
> (V.iv.85–93)

With everyone on stage waiting for the nuptials with which they are variously and deeply involved, the clown of the play will require all his skill if he is to hold atten-tion and please his audience, both on stage and off, with what is a complicated digression from the main business of the narrative. The few scripted on-stage responses do not help because, almost at the start, he has to justify the Duke's 'I like him very well', and a little later, provoke the surprised, 'By my faith, he is very swift and senten-tious' (V.iv.52 and 60–1). Having set up Touchstone to give a top-class performance, Jaques and the Duke then invite the audience to have second thoughts about their laughter:

> JAQUES   Is not this a rare fellow, my lord? He's as good
>   at any thing, and yet a fool.
> DUKE   He uses his folly like a stalking-horse, and
>   under the presentation of that he shoots his wit.
>
> (ll. 98–101)

They do not identify the prey this fowler has been aiming at from behind the screen of his folly, leaving that for the audience to recognize.

If we are to understand this episode in theatrical terms the text has to be read with an understanding of the time when it was first performed. Shakespeare has played to the public he knew by making the fool's conspicuously placed show-piece both topical and immediately relevant to the audience's daily lives. Announcing that he will speak of a 'quarrel' and the 'degrees' of quarrelling, Touchstone identifies a subject of current and urgent concern, especially in the city of London. For 'men of honour', a quarrel would be grounds for the 'mortal arbitrement' of a duel,[1] and 'to give the lie' (or *mentitia*), a matter of life or death.[2] Lodowick Bryskett's *Discourse of Civil Life* of 1603 declared:

> It is a so great a shame to be accounted a liar, that any other injury is cancelled by giving the lie, and he that receiveth it standeth so charged in his honour and reputation, that he cannot disburden himself of that imputation but by the striking of him that hath so given it, or by challenging him the combat.[3]

At the end of the sixteenth century many reasonable people accepted this dangerous protocol because the duel was an ordered and more civilized replacement of the 'killing affrays', ambushes, and assassinations to which injured persons would previously resort when the law proved unable to salve their honour and punish their adversaries. Duelling was also favoured because it was thought to encourage the 'manly' virtues of courage, alertness, strength, and expertise. These arguments were advanced with increasing confidence, for example by John Seldon in *The Duello, or Single Combat* (1610), but persons unskilled in sword-play continued to heed the biblical injunctions against the private pursuit of revenge. The virtues of the Italian *duello* were strongly contested and in 1613 its practice was outlawed by a royal *Proclamation against Private Challenges and Combats*.

Subsequently, persons wishing to settle quarrels by duel would leave the country to fight on Calais Sands or in the Netherlands. At the time when Touchstone was joking about the deadly and fashionable procedures of duelling, arguments on both sides were at their height and widely canvassed. Publishers, as well as the players, responded to public interest with William Segar's *The Book of Honour and Arms* (1590), *Giacomo di Grassi his True Art of Defence* (1594), *Vincentio Saviolo his Practice. In two Books. The first intreating of the use of the rapier and dagger. The second, of honour and honorable quarrels* (1594 and 1595), and George Silver, *Paradoxes of Defence* (1599).

The show-stopping comic performance at the very climax of *As You Like It* drew on topical issues that would have registered keenly with the great majority of an audience who had to walk home after dark through the un-lighted streets of London or had serious doubts about the administration of justice. The loss of this topical interest in present-day performance sets problems for the actor and threatens to unsettle the comedy's conclusion. But an Elizabethan clown's skills were physical as well as wittily verbal. To hold attention and raise a laugh, Touchstone's physical performance could show a sense of danger as he talks of quarrelling, or, perhaps, show an extreme cowardice. The text also gives opportunity to mime an encounter with an imaginary courtier who is fearsomely punctilious and bloodthirsty. A strong and eccentric physical presence and silent sight-gags were as much part of an Elizabethan clown's language as the words of a text and they are still talents that can speak directly to an audience even when the words to be spoken have lost much of their meaning and topicality.

The comedy is also removed from the twenty-first century when Touchstone, 'the clownish fool' (I.iii.126), claims to have picked a quarrel with 'a certain courtier' (V.iv.67–8) and boasts that they drew swords against each other. For those in the audience who daily experienced discrimination on grounds of class the joke would have been pointed because duels were the privileged recourse of the upper classes. Swordsmen 'concerned with the code of honour' were advised to 'ignore challenges among rustics' and the same principle held for disputes with tradesmen.[4] Touchstone was entering a closed social circle to which he very obviously did not belong; elsewhere he is called 'the roynish clown' (II.ii.8) by those who disapprove of him, meaning that he is 'scurvy, coarse, mean, paltry, base' or, in other words, a contemptible nonentity. His assumption of gentility, which had started with his 'salutation' on joining the well-connected assembly (V.iv.38, 55), would only serve to emphasize his lack of class. Here again, in present-day performances, physical comedy can dispel some of the verbal fog that has gathered since the script lost its topicality.

Laughter could either be *at* the stupidity of the low-born fellow behaving above his station, or *with* the licensed fool as he mocks the behaviour of his betters. When the comedy was first played, Robert Armin was the clown of the Chamberlain's Men, and would have been a Touchstone small in body and naturally grotesque in features. He was given roles that required him to act in the manner of a dog, sparrow, or frog, and may well have been cast as Shakespeare's Thersites, a 'botch of nature' who refuses to fight (*Troilus*, V.i.5). He was not famed for jigs, like his immediate predecessor, William Kemp, so he probably lacked the dexterity needed for the 'noble' swordsmanship to which Touchstone pretends.[5] Armin publicly claimed Richard Tarlton as his mentor, the famous clown who had preceded Kemp and whose face was alone sufficiently funny to set an audience laughing. Both Tarlton and Armin would often play rustic and clumsy characters, Tarlton's in particular being 'the ugliest, poorest and stupidest member of the community' who would be called upon to imitate the grandest in the land by becoming 'Lord of Misrule'.[6] The fact that Armin was confronting and imitating a courtier fixated on his honour would be enough to set an audience laughing.

Talk of a duel to be fought with swords might have been inserted into *As You Like It* as a specific allusion to Tarlton since the earlier clown had been given the title of 'Master Swordsman'. In his case, this was probably an honorific title that allowed him to preside as 'Sponsor' in the prize demonstrations that from the 1570s onwards were sometimes played in public theatres. We know that he officiated for a contest at the Bel Savage theatre just before his death in 1588.[7] With a nod to his master's reputation, Armin might extravagantly and inadequately mime the flourishes of swordplay, as if he were a gentleman born. When speaking of the retort, reply, reproof and countercheck, he might summon whatever physical dignity his short body and clown's features could muster. Certainly, at one point, Touchstone is very aware of physical appearance: noticing that his bride-to-be is not performing with the same propriety as himself, he reproves her with 'bear your body more seeming, Audrey' (V.iv.66). The goatherd has no verbal answer to this but a silent response could set off a series of physical interactions between the two ill-suited aspirants to gentility.

Despite active performances, audiences in later centuries are bound to miss much of the verbal bite in Touchstone's comic performance and this loss is the more serious because it reaches beyond this apparently extraneous episode and throws the conclusion of the entire comedy off its course. While laughter should still be subsiding, Shakespeare introduces an entry for Hymen, a new and unexpected addition to the *dramatis personae*. As he leads Rosalind and Celia on to the stage for their weddings, the '*Still music*' called for in the Folio text[8] emphasizes that this is an entirely new element in the play. Holding centre-stage, Touchstone has spoken of an 'If' as the 'only peace-maker' between two men on the point of fighting each other, and now a god takes his place to speak, in a very different voice, of another kind of peace-making:

> Then is there mirth in heaven,
> When earthly things made even
> Atone together.

(V.iv.102–4)

Hymen commands attention but his words are strange and ambiguous. *Atone* would not usually be used of love and weddings but of reconciliation or appeasement between two opposed and belligerent parties. *Mirth* in religious contexts could mean 'joy', and recent editors have noted an allusion here to the Gospel of Luke, 15.10: 'There is joy in the presence of the angels of God for one sinner that converteth.' Following so much laughter, however, the word's more everyday senses of 'fun, merriment, pleasure' might also register and, perhaps, be the dominant meaning at first. *Things* is a tricky word: in the plural it meant 'affairs, business, concerns' but, in association with *made even*, it might also refer to 'that which has been done, previous acts or deeds'. In association with *heaven* and *earthly*, it could also mean 'human beings'.[9] For Shakespeare's contemporaries, who seemed to have enjoyed riddles more than we do, the surprise of Hymen's entry and the ambiguities and unusual meanings of his opening words would have established a pause in the forward impetus of the play and encouraged thought backwards to its beginning and to certain intertwining themes that had only recently re-surfaced, to the delight of the audience, in Touchstone's verbal and physical comedy. Touchstone and Hymen are two sides of the one dramatic coin. As Touchstone raises laughter in which the whole audience shares, he is preparing a willing acceptance for Hymen's mysterious presence and oracular speech.

Both aspects of the one situation reflect earlier episodes in the comedy. The need to 'atone' or risk being killed, which is a subject for the clown's jokes and is echoed in the god's announcement, had been evoked at the start of the play in Oliver's tyranny over Orlando, his younger brother, and the tyranny of Duke Frederick over his brother, who has been forced into exile. Death had been threatened by the entry of Charles the wrestler. Having broken the ribs of three brothers off stage, he prepares to deal in the same way with Orlando and, when the amateur wrestler has thrown the professional, Charles is carried off as if dead. Once the action moves to the Forest of Arden, there is talk of killing deer, the 'citizens' of the forest, and, later, of a poisonous snake and hungry lioness, both threatening death. With a song and procession in celebration of a successful hunt, death is visually represented by the deer's bloody skin worn in triumph by the victor. Death also makes several brief metaphoric entries, for example when Touchstone speaks of wit that is not appreciated:

> When a man's verses cannot be understood, nor a man's good wit seconded with the forward child understanding, it strikes a man more dead than a great reckoning in a little room.[10]
>
> (III.iii.9–12)

When Celia reports that Orlando lies 'stretch'd along like a wounded knight', using mortal combat as a metaphor for sexual engagement, Rosalind immediately thinks of death, replying that 'he comes to kill my heart' (III.ii.225–6 and 231–2).

Hymen's entry, with his claim to heavenly authority, total command of the stage, and 'wedlock-hymn' (V.iv. 131), follows immediately after the spectacle of Touchstone's comic pretension, which has reminded the audience of social order and conformity. The two contrasting performances reflect aspects of earlier episodes: the decorum that is observed whenever either of the two dukes is present, and the mocking of social hierarchies in the clown's encounters with almost everyone he meets, especially those he considers his inferiors, Sir Oliver Martext, the hedge priest, and William, the shepherd, whom he baffles with condescension and pretentious words. Social status has been abused by Orlando's 'servitude' in his own home (I.i.1–22) and by Oliver's treatment of Adam, his old servant. In contrast, Adam's selfless service to Orlando exemplifies:

> The constant service of the antique world,
> When service sweat for duty, not for meed
>
> (II.iii.57ff.)

As the comedy approaches its conclusion, social order and disorder are both present in lively and enjoyable form when two young pages sing, 'like two gypsies on a horse', in celebration of adult mating in the spring time as 'the only pretty ring time' (V.iii). Touchstone complains that 'the note was very untuneable' but the singers are deaf to his criticism. All disharmony is dissipated when Hymen enters and yet, as everyone on stage begins to respond, he interrupts to insist on harmony:

> Peace, ho! I bar confusion;
> 'Tis I must make conclusion
> Of these most strange events.... .
>
> (V.iv.119ff.)

When Hymen calls for choral singing to honour wedlock as the 'blessed bond of board and bed' and 'great Juno's crown', he is echoing the Book of Common Prayer, which repeatedly asserts that the 'holy state of matrimony' was ordained by God for the good of man and woman.

Like many jokes in Shakespeare's comedies, such tight knots of meaning and multiple allusions have dated very seriously and must be carefully unravelled before they can be understood and appreciated today. When introduced with a procession and solemn music, as they are here, or when emphasized by repetition and a variety of on-stage reactions, as again they are here, they will attract a watchful attention from present-day audiences and yet remain less effective than they were at first because of the changes in language, social habits, and mental attitudes that time has brought about. As with the jokes, it is the non-verbal elements of performance that are best able to keep the play on its original course. Even if words are only partly understood, the contrast that Touchstone's verbal sparring and clown's physique make with Hymen's unearthly appearance and oracular utterance will always register immediately on both ear and eye, especially since they follow each other in commanding attention on a crowded stage. Later, in the last moments of the comedy, when Jaques speaks to each of the bridegrooms in turn, a strong visual focus is brought to bear on both members of each couple so that unscripted and physical reactions will be their last contributions to the narrative. Made clearly and freely, according to the imagination, invention, skill and personality of each actor, these non-verbal responses will be the culmination of the comedy, tuned to whatever response the audience may have made. After Jaques has left the stage, everyone joins together in 'rustic revelry' (l. 171), a dance that expresses physically whatever mutual happiness each very different couple enjoys after all the comedy's 'strange' events.

* * *

The reason why Shakespeare's comedies remain so broadly popular can scarcely lie in their jokes relating to defunct social customs or in the intellectual cunning of their verbal wit. While these attractions have faded, the one aspect of all the comedies that, to this day, is almost sure to affect an audience is the opportunity they provide for imaginative and individually distinctive performances that speak directly to the senses of an audience, beyond the reach of words. The physical skills of Elizabethan clowns, their rapport with an audience, and their ability to improvise, could have given to a battery of words the fun of instantaneous and spirited engagement, no matter whether the text was fully understood or not. Armin was especially famous for extemporary exchanges with his audience, tackling any theme that was tossed to him. Even while staying faithful to Shakespeare's text, he would be able to turn his performance into a game of connivance and interplay with his audience. The timing and pointing of speech could be adjusted to the mood in which it was being received and his performance rides on any tide of laughter that united spectators. Gestures and wordless exclamations could answer, emphasize, or undercut any vocal response the audience made. As Touchstone, his very presence would speak constantly for the 'rare fellow'

who is 'good at anything and yet a fool'. He had only to
pause, or look straight at a member of the audience, or
repeat a single word to turn a difficult speech to comedy.

Similar skills can bring performances alive today when
the shape of a theatre gives actors and audience close
contact with each other, even when words and activity are
far removed from those of contemporary life. A present-
day actor who is unfamiliar with the reality and formali-
ties of duelling but skilful in mime and quick in invention
would be able to make the danger and pretension underlying Touchstone's final performance physically apparent
and so bring its basic meaning across to his audience. In
rehearsal he might well get lost in the long sequence of
semi-technical terms and have to search his mind for what
was coming next, and so transmit a sense of triumph
when he did remember. Reproducing that experience in
performance, acting as if he were at his wit's end even
though he has mastered the text and is taking the solo
spot, he could seem to pluck success out of a fear of
failure and so, with a dose of self-mockery, remain close
to Shakespeare's text and revitalize meanings that might
otherwise have died.

When Shakespeare's words are at their simplest and
refer to activity that is common in life outside the
theatre at all times and in all places, the scope for an
actor's skill and imagination is especially wide and inviting. Histories of performance, and personal experience
of present-day performances, will show that these
moments have always been a source of an audience's
pleasure and its close involvement in the drama.
Examples can be found everywhere in Shakespeare's
plays but are especially numerous in the comedies with
their frequent asides, emphatic assertions, and sudden
revelations that positively encourage improvisation and
close contact with an audience. In his day, moreover, a
strong critical tradition distinguished comedy from
tragedy on account of its closeness to off-stage life as well
as by the absence of death in its narratives. However im-
probable the plot and witty the *dramatis personae*, a line
of scholars and authors, from Aristotle and Cicero to Sir

Philip Sidney and Ben Jonson, were agreed that a comedy should be an imitation of life and a mirror of social behaviour. Jonson called for:

> . . . deeds and language such as men do use,
> And persons such as Comedy would choose,
> When she would show an image of the times,
> And sport with human follies, not with crimes.[11]

Such views may partly account for the frequent allusions to lived experience in Shakespeare's comedies that are now lost on audiences and readers, but they also encouraged a style of writing that was closer to the accents and simplicities of everyday talk than the 'high' and thought-packed speeches that were considered appropriate for tragedy. Shakespeare's comedies are full of short speeches, and some longer ones, that are both easy to understand and open for an actor to use in whatever way seems most appropriate to the moment as the drama changes from performance to performance.

When Touchstone holds the stage at the end of *As You Like It*, several opportunities of this kind occur. Speaking of Audrey to the Duke as 'A poor virgin, sir, an ill-favour'd thing, sir, but mine own', the actor is free to choose the feeling and thought that provokes each one of those simple phrases. 'Mine own', for example, can be proud, apologetic, smug, enigmatic, or sexually suggestive. If Touchstone looks directly at Audrey on the conclusion of these words or if she turns away from him at this moment, the feeling and subsequent laughter will be very different. So, too, if she has heard all that he has said, or if he has made sure she has not. They would also be different if he had become oblivious of her presence as soon as he started to speak about her to his superior, the Duke, and only now remembers that she is there. What happens on stage at this moment is likely to be largely improvised, especially if Audrey, while holding her tongue, responds physically in any assertive manner, whether of pleasure, petulance, or incipient rebellion. Similarly, the conclusion of Touchstone's account of the degrees of the lie – 'Your If is the only peace-maker; much virtue in If' – is simple enough verbally to be played in many different ways. It can be confident, careless, deeply serious, mockingly serious, or downright cowardly. Its last four words can carry a message different from the first half of the sentence, with Touchstone finishing in triumph, mock piety, self-satisfaction, or, perhaps, with an air of mystery as if keeping deeper secrets to himself.

Because his imagination was physical and sensuous Shakespeare's plays exist beyond the reach of words or half-hidden within them. In response, actors are led by their imaginations to speak with bodily presence and physical action as well as with words, and *how* they speak becomes as significant as *what* they speak. Members of an audience will then be witnesses to events on stage that are images of life to which they can respond naturally and almost unconsciously, without the aid of verbalized thought, and avoiding many of the difficulties brought about with the passage of time. They find themselves free to use their imaginations and make their own sense of what happens on stage. And in studying the texts, readers can do much the same if they try to imagine how words, actions, and the persons of the play could be brought to life.

* * *

Short and simple speeches that are able to trigger highly individual and telling moments of performance are found everywhere in the comedies, and usually bring laughter with them. A little more than half way through *As You Like It*, while Rosalind is pretending to be the young Ganymede, the verbally simple exchanges that she shares with Orlando are all charged with whatever sensations the two bring to the encounter and almost any speech is liable to be greeted with the audience's laughter:

ROSALIND   … ask me what you will, I will grant it.
ORLANDO Then love me, Rosalind.

ROSALIND Yes, faith, will I, Fridays and Saturdays, and all.
ORLANDO And wilt thou have me?
ROSALIND Ay, and twenty such.
ORLANDO What sayest thou?
ROSALIND Are you not good?
ORLANDO I hope so.
ROSALIND Why then, can one desire too much of a good thing?

(IV.i.100–9)

No dictionary or historical research is needed to elucidate any of these words, and actors can take advantage of this clarity to show the person they play at full stretch, whether secure, fearful, impatient, indulgent, or somewhere between mockery and sober seriousness. The mood can change quickly or remain constant; voices can vary in volume and the text can be pointed in many different ways. For example, a pause can come after Rosalind's 'Ay',[12] and then 'and twenty such' follow quickly to cover up an instinctive response that had almost led her to say too much. Alternatively, all four words might be said slowly as she tries to maintain her role as Ganymede while tenderly relishing the contact this gives with Orlando, not recovering her full disguise until he has responded. Or both can enjoy the game and give provocatively sexual meanings to *have, good, desire* and *thing*. They could remain at a distance from each other or move progressively closer. Momentarily, they might touch and then withdraw. Mutual sexual awareness can grow with the words or go far beyond them. Perhaps both persons, alone or together, break into brief laughter at the absurdity of it all, or out of happiness.

When placed at a significant exit, a short and simple speech may not be capable of any great variety of feeling but invite a flourish that expresses an access of confidence or excitement and sustains a climax by focusing attention on the actor's physical presence. For example, in *Much Ado About Nothing* when Constable Dogberry has been asked to examine 'two aspicious persons', he can leave the stage exuding self-importance as he calls upon Verges, his assistant headborough, to 'meet me at the gaol'. When incriminating evidence has been obtained at the trial, Dogberry concludes the scene with the cry, 'O that I had been writ down an ass!' and probably leaves the stage after striking a heroic or frustrated posture. On his final exit from the play, having been rewarded for his efforts, he has a series of simple exclamations, starting with the respectful 'God save the foundation!' and running on to the curt or, perhaps, magnanimous order to Verges, 'Come, neighbour' (III.v.59–60, IV.ii.85–6, and V.i.303–11). Having gained the focus of attention by speaking these not very remarkable words, an inventive comic actor can use any one short phrase to encapsulate his entire performance and win a last laugh from his audience.

The verbal simplicity that frequently raises a laugh may also be used to other effect. In *Much Ado*, Benedick has a number of brief and unexpected speeches that are funnier than he intends and yet so self-revealing that an audience's laughter may be held back by the deeper feelings that are exposed. For example, 'This can be no trick', at the start of a soliloquy, is funny because it goes against everything the audience has just witnessed but it also reveals that, against his will, Benedick has been touched to the point of blindness by hearing that Beatrice loves him passionately. His decisive 'I will go get her picture' as he leaves the stage is funny because it shows that his mind is now so full of Beatrice that he must do something about it; it is affecting because, in her absence, he would be happy if he only had her picture[13] – for an Elizabethan, a more difficult substitute to 'go get' than a modern photograph to use as a pin-up (II.iii.201–2 and 243). When, at their wedding, Claudio denounces Hero as a whore, Benedick's 'This looks not like a nuptial' is probably spoken as an awkward joke to cover a deeper concern for both groom and bride; it may also be used to defy anyone else to laugh. The three words, 'Strike up, pipers!' with which Benedick concludes the play and calls everyone to join in a dance can be a comically urgent attempt to prevent Beatrice from talking any more.

Alternatively, they could be a confident brushing aside of other business or a triumphant over-brimming of happiness. Together with an energized physical presence they might express a confident sexuality, the exact quality of the bawdy joke depending on how the role has developed throughout the play and how Beatrice responds to him at this time. The entire performance of the role can be summed up as these three simple words provoke laughter and cause everyone on stage and in the audience to respond in his and her own way.

Speeches that are simply phrased as if to raise laughter will sometimes express deeply felt or, even, dangerous feelings that have previously been hidden. In *The Merchant of Venice* when Shylock has lost both daughter and ducats and been mercilessly taunted by Solanio and Salerio, he parts from his fellow Jew at the end of the highly charged scene, with: 'Go, Tubal, and meet me at our synagogue; go, good Tubal; at our synagogue, Tubal' (III.i.114–16). Repetition that elsewhere would invite comically varied emphasis or an equally funny stumbling or dithering, could here enable an actor to vary the deep emotions experienced by Shylock or develop the power of a single emotion that now totally possesses him. The simple words can express Shylock's passionate desire for vengeance, his hurt or avarice, his feeling for an only daughter and dead wife, or his devotion to race or religion. They may be spoken with increasing confidence, frustration, apprehension, or panic. The act of leaving the stage will extend further whatever effect he has made, his steps being rapid through passion or slowly measured in determination or, perhaps, satisfaction. At this moment, Shylock's stature may seem to grow formidably or be diminished by rabid hatred. Some actors have added a solemn and ritualistic prayer on the exit, others a savage curse. Here, and elsewhere in this play, the text is so open to different interpretations that Shylock can become – and in a few productions, he has become[14] – the butt of cruel and inhuman racism, a passionate villain, or a pitiable egotist.

When Shylock leaves the stage for the last time, having been thwarted in revenge and publicly humiliated in a court of law, he has a small sequence of short phrases, as Dogberry has in *Much Ado*. The first – 'I am content' – is the briefest and most open to different enactments, ranging in feeling through quietly controlled irony to proud reticence, fatalistic submission, or tortured inability to say more:

> PORTIA   Art thou contented, Jew? What dost thou say?
> SHYLOCK I am content.
> PORTIA   Clerk, draw a deed of gift.
> SHYLOCK I pray you, give me leave to go from hence;
>   I am not well; send the deed after me
>   And I will sign it.

(IV.i.388–92)

A reader, alerted to the potential of such simple words, may identify with Shylock in this exchange or be appalled at his attempt to cut off a pound of Antonio's living flesh. When studying the text, sufficient time can be taken to explore a range of possible performances and reactions to them. In the theatre at this final moment, an audience may well receive an inescapable and unforgettable impression as the actor varies the sensation with each of the five short phrases or builds a single emotion towards a verbally restrained and deeply felt climax. Shylock's bearing, his taking of breath as he turns to leave, and his steps across the stage will all receive the closest attention from other persons on stage and in the audience. Not responding to Gratiano's accompanying taunts, he maintains a prolonged silence as he makes the exit. So confident was Laurence Olivier that the audience would be sympathizing with him, that he concluded his performance with a howl of pain that was released only when he was off stage and out of sight.[15]

In both these instances a simply worded speech that concludes a scene of strong dramatic interest will play on an audience's emotions rather than move them to laughter. On other occasions a few words may well do both, as, for instance, Antonio's last speech in *The Merchant*. This is not on his exit, since he will leave with others later,[16] but it comes at a moment when all attention is focused on him, immediately after Portia has welcomed him to Belmont and given him a letter with the news that three of his argosies, previously reported to be lost at sea, are 'richly come to harbour suddenly'. Having listened in silence, he says only, 'I am dumb', which he could speak as if too happy to think of adequate words, or as a joke to express his wonder at the 'strange accident' that has re-stored his fortunes (V.1.273–9). On the other hand, the three words could be a point-blank refusal to say more. Antonio had financed Bassanio's successful journey as suitor to this rich heiress and may now feel isolated as he mourns the loss of his own 'dear' friend for whose life he had offered to give his own. He may have no feeling left to welcome the recovery of his wealth. By his manner of speech and physical bearing, perhaps by a gesture or turning away, an actor might be able to make an obvious joke and also reveal deep emotion.

* * *

Laughter in Shakespeare's plays can be simple or almost mindless, but usually it is more complicated. He was aware that a 'wild laughter' could outface the pain and fears of death and that sometimes 'wit makes wise things foolish'. In his plays, folly is often close to madness and fast-moving comic action can seem like the 'fierce vexation of a dream'. His clowns are liable to be melancholy and to 'care for something' that is hidden from other people, in at least one instance being driven by what the clown's 'poor body … requires'.[17] Occasionally Shakespeare ridiculed the behaviour of 'mortals', so that we might be thought to 'play the fools with the time, and the spirits of the wise sit in the clouds and mock us'.[18]

To understand how laughter is provoked and managed on any one occasion we must study the way the actors perform and how their performance is experienced in a theatre. The words of the text itself remain constant but the effect of what is spoken will be different on each occasion. An entire theatrical event has to be taken into account: the social and political context in which the play is produced, the ways in which it was rehearsed and then staged, who the actors are and what skills they possess. How an audience sees and hears the play matters too, and this will be influenced by whatever interests and immediate concerns it brings to the theatre. Because theatre provides a progressive experience over an interval of time – the actors' performances developing and changing and the audience's response growing wider or more subtle, more intense or, perhaps, more frustrated – what the play achieves at any one moment must also be considered in the light of what has gone before. This huge task can best be started on a narrow front in the hope that scrutiny of a small sample of text may open up the complexity of one moment and some of the long-term effects of the play in performance.

To take one example in the place of many, consider a short speech from Beatrice's encounter with Benedick after Claudio has denounced Hero in public on their wedding day: 'O God, that I were a man! I would eat his heart in the market-place' (*Much Ado About Nothing*, IV.i.303–4). The only words that would cause the slightest difficulty to a modern reader or actor are 'in the market-place'. In Shakespeare's day, this was a public place much as it is now, but members of a family such as Hero's would not go there in the ordinary course of events. They did not leave home to shop or barter for themselves since tradesmen would come to them[19] or to their servants. Nor would they choose to walk alone through such a place of public resort, no matter whether it was crowded or deserted.[20] 'In the market-place' might well be Beatrice's after-thought, a humiliation she piles on top of the horrendous fantasy of cannibalism. The whole assertion is so far from any possible reality that she may seem to be going out of her mind, for how does one 'eat' a heart, by what means get hold of it, leave alone consume it? If Beatrice speaks rationally, she is being purposefully grotesque or flippantly provocative, not intending any real threat by what she says. In whatever way 'would eat his heart' is spoken and that moment acted, a further question is why her imagination should lead her to think of a fully public display in the midst of the ordinary business of people about whom she can know very little. 'In the market-place' could be the last flourish of a flight of fantasy or the nailing down of her thoughts to a bizarre but everyday reality.

Before reaching any conclusion about how to deal with these out-of-date matters, the actor will have made other choices or instinctive decisions. When she exclaims 'O God', Beatrice may be aware that she is in a church or chapel and so speak with reverence, or, less deliberately, she might be using a readily available form of words. The second part of 'O God, that I were a man!' is verbally very simple but for Beatrice, on any literal level, the wish is impossible, so that actors are free to imagine whatever they sense is right and act accordingly. In practice, the moment has been played in ways as various as the personalities, instincts, and physiques of those performing the role. Fervent prayer, unthinking fury, exasperated exclamation, cold calculation, and reasoned statement of a long-held preference are among the alternatives that might be adopted. Having failed to come to terms with the harm that Claudio has done to her close and very dear cousin, Beatrice might be possessed by 'wild laughter' or wide awake in the grip of a nightmare. Both actors will have to choose what to do while Beatrice is speaking these words. Does she look very directly at Benedick, the only other person present and the man to whom her mind and feelings are now committed? If she squares up to him, perhaps coming towards him, how does he respond? Does he look away, baffled by what he hears, or is he so alarmed that he reaches for his sword? Whatever happens between the two of them as Beatrice says she wishes to be a man, the idea of eating a man's heart follows directly, as if she is now released from all conventional thoughts. Perhaps Benedick and his heart have displaced Claudio in her mind.

How quickly, slowly, evenly, uninterruptedly, do the various phrases of this short sentence follow each other?

At what volume and tempo are words spoken? What is the dominant emotion of Beatrice here? Much will depend on the instincts of both actors with regard to gender and sexuality, violence and injustice, fantasy and rationality, and on the response of their audience. Questions multiply but we can gain a degree of certainty by considering the moment in relation to what has happened beforehand, most obviously only seconds previously when Beatrice had already wished she were a man. At that time she said no more, as if the enormity of what Claudio had done had left her with no other thought or feeling than the need to revenge as a man would revenge when faced with such a wrong. However, a minute or two before this, words had been charged with great and contrasted feelings: she had declared her love for Benedick and, with the next breath, asked him to fight her enemy and kill him:

BEATRICE … I was about to protest I loved you.
BENEDICK And do it with all thy heart?
BEATRICE I love you with so much of my heart that none is left to protest.
BENEDICK Come, bid me do anything for thee.
BEATRICE Kill Claudio.
BENEDICK Ha! not for the wide world.
BEATRICE You kill me to deny it. Farewell.

(IV.i.282ff.)

The two words 'Kill Claudio' are famous in the stage history of the play for expressing varying degrees of unreasoned passion, precise and lethal feeling, outrageous mockery, or awareness of absurdity, and also for provoking laughter, either intentionally or inadvertently. It is this highly volatile exchange that prepares for the first 'O God, that I were a man!' and also for its repetition and amplification seconds later. Study of the sequence of earlier speeches and actions shows that in committing herself to the fantastic unreality of 'eat his heart in the market-place', Beatrice displaces Benedick from her mind and takes upon herself the unlawful act of vengeance. Her passion and imagination have led her to thoughts more crude and bloody than those of any man of honour. In a moment she recognizes a frightening truth about herself.

By this time Beatrice is involved in the same real-life concerns about duelling as Touchstone at the end of *As You Like It*, but her nightmare instincts are fuelled by a far more passionate sense of injustice and personal helplessness in the face of society's failure to keep the peace. Again, by considering earlier exchanges the present moment can be clarified. These fierce feelings are a development of the 'skirmish of wit' and 'merry war' in which she and Benedick have been engaged from the start of the play. The two actors will have to choose whether the later violence grows out of those earlier contests and was implicit in them, or whether the wished-for killing of Claudio expresses more desperate or more sexual instincts than the 'merry' warfare. When Benedick had said that talking with Beatrice was like standing 'at a mark with a whole army shooting at me', he may have sensed a violence within Beatrice which, at that time, had found only a guarded or disguised expression. The sexual, social, and moral issues that, a few years later, were to drive the dramatic action of *The Tragedy of Othello, Moor of Venice* may have found an earlier footing in this comedy, where they are presented as if they were 'much ado about nothing'.

All earlier verbal allusions to conflict and mastery prepare for 'O God, that I were a man! I would eat his heart in the market-place' and tracing them can bring that moment into sharper focus. They also indicate how much depends on the identity and skills of the actors and on their performance throughout the play in all its accidental and improvised detail, whether they have made their presences felt with accumulating force and how their imaginations have given a progressive semblance of reality to the persons of the play. The moment now being considered can draw members of an audience closer to what is happening on stage and to each other or it can alert and unsettle them. It may awaken real-life concerns, so that some members of the audience become closer in sympathy with the persons of the play. Or the ferocity of the confrontation may establish a distance between spectators and the on-stage behaviour, so that they watch in superior understanding; if they laugh it will be to mock those who 'play the fools with the time'. Alternatively, the stress of instinctive, half-conscious thoughts and distorted, half-formulated passions can awaken pity for these two persons who find themselves in thrall to each other. In these ways, studying the theatrical potential of one moment will raise questions about the meaning and theatrical potential of the entire text. Was it written to explore the connection between violence and sexuality, or to show the social and political conditioning of relations between women and men? Or did Shakespeare want us to laugh at inherited competitive instincts, the inherent clumsiness of verbal communication, or the dangers of romantic idealism when put to the test of action?

* * *

This study of Shakespeare's comedies has moved repeatedly between the text, an actor's possible use of it, and an audience's experience. This is potentially confusing but also necessary if the plays are to be considered in the form for which they were written. Besides, as a reader becomes accustomed to these changes of attention, a play comes more alive in the mind and has a freshness comparable to that experienced in a good performance. The difficulty of understanding some of the language and accounting for the changes in meaning that the passage of time has brought encourages actors to rely more on physical performance, and study does well to follow this lead and visualize what is happening on every occasion as thoroughly and carefully as words are considered and their operation analysed.

In study of the comedies, the simplest passages in a text call for particularly close attention. Even at crucial moments in the dramatic action – and this may be a mark of those that will prove most crucial in performance – the writing is often particularly simple and free, generously giving actors the opportunity to take over the play by tuning it very precisely to their own imaginations, talents and stage presences, and in response to their audience. What can be studied is the potential for performance at a crucial stage in the action, and the contribution it makes to the audience's progressive experience of the play.

A start can be made by identifying a few simple words in a context where the speaker is alone or the centre of attention, and then speaking them aloud in a number of ways, varying quite arbitrarily the tempo, emphasis, volume, and phrasing of speech. This free-ranging practical experiment will serve to identify a number of possible deliveries, after which the next step would be to imagine the moment being acted. It may help to see it with a well-known actor cast in the role and then question why he or she should say each particular word, and ask what action might accompany them and how the body would be held and where the eyes are looking. Then everyone else who is on stage should be considered, imagining what expectations they might bring and what reactions would follow. Finally, the audience's expectations and responses need to be brought into this imaginary event. Having started in the present time, study can then explore what meanings and implications the words and accompanying actions would have had in Shakespeare's day, which now are lost. Slowly – because this is a complicated matter – the possibilities for laughter can be reviewed and the entire play will begin to perform itself in the imagination according to an individual involvement with its language, persons, settings, and action.

Notes

1. *Twelfth Night*, III.iv.249; see also ll. 209–39, and *Hamlet*, I.iii.66–8.
2. On duelling, see Fredrick R. Bryson, *The Sixteenth-Century Italian Duel* (Chicago: University of Chicago Press, 1938), especially pp. 20 and 58; and Robert Baldick, *The Duel: A History of Duelling* (London: Chapman & Hall, 1965).
3. Among the authorities quoted in Baldick, *The Duel*, Chapter III, 'The Duel of Honour'.
4. See Bryson, *The Sixteenth-Century Italian Duel*, p. 20.
5. See David Wiles's account of Armin's roles in *Shakespeare's Clown: Actor and Text in the Elizabethan Playhouse* (Cambridge: Cambridge University Press, 1987), chapter 10. Juliet Dusinberre has argued that Touchstone's encounter with Sir Oliver Martext shows that he was played by Kemp and not Armin (see *In Arden: Editing Shakespeare* [London: Thomson, 2003], pp. 239–51), but a recollection of Kemp would suit the scene as well, if not better, as assigning the role to him. The encounter with William, a less quick-witted clown, and the weariness of Touchstone's legs on arrival in Arden (see II.iv.2–3) are among other factors that argue that Armin was the clown of *As You Like It*.
6. Wiles, *Shakespeare's Clown*, pp. 20–3.
7. See Herbert Berry, *The Noble Science: A Study and Transcription of Sloane Ms. 2530, Papers of the Masters of Defence of London, Temp. Henry VIII to 1590* (Newark and London: Associated University Presses, 1991), pp. 3–8.
8. The Folio, the sole early text, has a number of stage directions indicating that the printer's copy was the author's manuscript, or a copy of it, prepared for use in the theatre; see, for example, Michael Hattaway's edition for Cambridge University Press (Cambridge, 2000), pp. 201–3.
9. See, for example, *Macbeth*, V.iv.13.
10. Another reference to lived experience that is not readily understood today. This was once thought to be a reference to the death of Christopher Marlowe in a tavern at Deptford. The more recent assumption is that Touchstone speaks of what happened when someone had drunk more than could be paid for. Agnes Latham's suggestion that it is a clown's obscene joke is likely to be at least part of Touchstone's meaning (New Arden edition [1975], pp. xxxiii–iv).
11. Ben Jonson, *Every Man in His Humour*, Prologue, ll. 21–4.
12. The comma printed here reproduces the punctuation of the original Folio text, but has little authority since Shakespeare's

punctuation could have been modified by both scribe and compositor.

13. Or, in the words of Bassanio in *The Merchant of Venice*, to feed on the shadow instead of the substance (III.ii.126–9).

14. An excellent account of Shylock on the stage is to be found in M. M. Mahood's edition of *The Merchant of Venice* (Cambridge: Cambridge University Press, 1987), pp. 42–52, and in its continuation by Charles Edelmann in the 'updated edition' of 2003, pp. 57–65. Of exceptional interest is Wilhelm Hortmann's account of Shylock in *Shakespeare on the German Stage: The Twentieth Century* (Cambridge: Cambridge University Press, 1998), pp. 254–6 and 421–2.

15. See, for example, the Cambridge edition, p. 50.

16. See below, Chapter 3, pp. 71–4.

17. *Love's Labour's Lost*, V.ii.843 and 374; *A Midsummer Night's Dream*, IV.i.66; *Twelfth Night*, III.i.26; and *All's Well that Ends Well*, I.iii.28.

18. *A Midsummer Night's Dream*, III.ii.115; and *2, Henry IV*, II.ii.135–7.

19. See, for example, *Taming of the Shrew*, IV.iii.52ff.

20. See, for example, *I, Henry VI*, I.iv.38ff.: Talbot tells how he was greeted with 'scoffs, and scorns, and contumelious taunts' when: 'In open market-place produc'd they me / To be a public spectacle to all… .'

2

Living with the Tragedies:
a Progressive Experience

Shakespeare's tragedies are both the most accessible and the most formidable of his plays. One or two persons dominate each of them as their story provides the main action and the principal focus for our attention. In the comedies we cannot be so sure, as the action shifts from one set of persons to another and to a different part of the forest, another city, a more private room, or out into the street. The history plays are structured in much the same way as the comedies, but after *Titus Andronicus* the tragedies are more consistently focused on one story-line. Even when the scene moves from Scotland to England in *Macbeth* or from Egypt to Rome in *Antony and Cleopatra*, the thrust of the drama remains constant and keeps us watching and waiting for what will happen to the protagonists. The sub-plot of *King Lear* would seem an exception to this, but the story of the Duke of Gloucester and his sons reflects that of Lear and his daughters in many ways and soon becomes interwoven with it: Gloucester dies off stage without preventing the tragedy coming to a full close. And yet, while we do not lose our bearings in any of the major tragedies, the journey we follow makes new demands at each stage of the way, and what happens so fully engages us that we may well want to pause to take breath or avert our eyes as we begin to fear the outcome.

All except the earliest tragedies occupy our attention deeply by giving palpable and recognizable form to un-

spoken misgivings and desires. We can often sense that
speech has the accent and pulse of thoughts that underlie the words. Instinctive impulses are betrayed within
what is consciously communicated so that more is said
than the speaker intends. In effect, the leading persons
of the tragedies have divided minds, in much the same
way as we may have. When we encounter them on stage
we are drawn to study their faces to gain a closer knowledge, as we might do with people encountered in daily
life. Returning to study the text a second or third time,
we find that they still retain secrets and hold our attention. By these means our imaginations are caught up in
daunting circumstances and, despite our very obvious differences, we seem to live with the protagonists. It is this
close and sustained involvement that renders the experience of seeing the tragedies so formidable.

* * *

Peering through the keyhole of a single line of text will
show the difficulties of studying Shakespeare's tragedies
in performance. For example, consider 'She should have
died hereafter' (*Macbeth*, V.v.17). How are those five
words spoken, or rather, how might an actor say them?
What does Macbeth think, at this moment, of the past
and future to which he obliquely refers? What compulsion motivates this speech? To whom, if anyone, does he
speak? And then, what is the effect of this moment on the
rest of the play? Why did Shakespeare have Lady Macbeth
die off stage at just this moment, when Macbeth has
defiantly commanded 'Hang out our banners on the
outward walls!' and yet cannot meet his opponents,
'dareful, beard to beard, / And beat them backward
home'? How much are his thoughts, as well as his actions,
driven by fate; how much by conscious choice? And, as
there is no one way for an actor to play this moment, so it
will be received in many different ways. How does any
particular audience experience Macbeth's sense of loss,
his pity, fear, love, amazement, or will-power? What does

this line of text and the acting of this moment contribute to the experience of witnessing *The Tragedy of Macbeth* in any one performance, or – far more difficult to assess – in all performances? How best can we study this play in performance?

A speech of still fewer words can exemplify the need to take everyone on stage into account and the stage itself, and not only concern ourselves with the hero of a tragedy. When Coriolanus is struck down by nameless conspirators, calling out 'Kill, kill, kill, kill, kill him!' (*Coriolanus*, V.vi.130), he is given no words to speak, so that an audience's concern for him is suddenly aborted, as if a gap has opened up in the very fabric of the tragedy. Some actors manage to die spectacularly. Laurence Olivier fell forward from an upper level of the stage and was caught by his feet so that he hung there like a lifeless corpse.[1] More commonly actors die facing the audience and are struck down from behind, so that something of the hero's reaction is briefly visible, perhaps accompanied by an inarticulate cry. Lesser persons in the scene, all but one of them nameless, remain on stage to urge restraint, express blame or sorrow, and remember those whom Coriolanus has 'widowed and unchilded'. With no words from the hero about his suffering, endurance, pride or ignorance, an audience is left to view the wordless spectacle and accept the event as best they can. A Volscian Lord tells those who watch on stage that they must 'make the best of it', and their reactions provide the last moments of the tragedy. This Lord's message is also appropriate for members of a theatre audience. Whatever accumulated residue remains of their earlier experiences will unconsciously inform the response that each individual makes to the last silent and static image of a Roman soldier and leader lying dead among a crowd of aliens. For these reasons, the effect of its entire action is relevant when studying the conclusion of this tragedy.

The focus of attention at the conclusion of *Macbeth* is also wide. The hero is no longer on stage but Macduff enters bearing what he calls the 'usurper's cursèd head' and then the whole assembled cast hails Malcolm as 'King of Scotland'. This much is clear, but when the young king replies with a single speech of sixteen lines, he is heard, for all the text tells us, in universal silence (V.viii.54–9). Whatever questions his followers might want to ask and whatever feelings his words provoke, the victor does not 'spend a large expense of time' in final reckonings (ll. 60–1). With almost shocking speed, all the thanes are created earls, restoration and punitive action are promised, 'grace' is requested from 'Grace' itself, thanks are given comprehensively, and a general invitation is extended to a coronation ceremony that will take place elsewhere. Those who surround the new centre of attention are likely to make some audible response and react physically at each point in this public address. Actors are almost sure to take the opportunity to improvise a few words. In present-day theatres, directors will clarify the outcome by specific and choreographed crowd reactions, light changes, and sound effects. While none of this is required or controlled by the text, something more is bound to happen when Malcolm's speech comes to an end. Then, after everyone has left the stage, Macbeth's head may remain, perhaps with blood still dropping from it. Or this stage property may have been carried out in triumph, high above other heads. It could be subjected to curses or further indignities but none of this is scripted. Shakespeare has ensured that the audience is left to make the best of it according to their experience of the entire play.

Nothing Malcolm says matches the self-awareness and sensitivity that has repeatedly marked the presence of Macbeth and Lady Macbeth from the start of the play and has intensified during the final Act. No suggestions of unspeakable feelings are given here, as they are, for example, in 'She should have died hereafter...'. Malcolm's concluding lines allow no time for reflection:

> ... this, and what needful else
> That calls upon us, by the grace of Grace,
> We will perform in measure, time, and place.

So thanks to all at once and to each one,
Whom we invite to see us crown'd at Scone.
                    Flourish   Exeunt Omnes.

Any access of understanding, recognition of deep-seated
feelings, devising of punishment, or detailed hopes for
social and political change will have to come from
members of the audience, who have shared in the terrible
events and thwarted hopes of the play's unfolding action.
In imagination, they have lived with this tragedy throughout its performance, at times being drawn to empathize
with both the protagonists, but now, at its end, the dramatist has left considered judgement and instinctive feeling
to them. He did not tell the actors what to say or do.
Malcolm does not even address the English soldiers who
have made invasion possible. No one has been given anything to say, while the audience watches everyone take up
an appropriate order and make the final *Exeunt*.

Study of this and other tragedies must pay attention to
the progressive experience of an audience that derives
from far more than the most potent of its words or any
statement of theme or argument. The whole process of
the action comes into the account: the passage of time
and the successive moments of expectation, surprise,
conflict, crisis or climax; sensations of peace or uncertainty; feelings that are not verbally expressed and actions
with motives that are not verbally explained. These elements are not easily studied because they are bound to
vary from production to production, performance to performance, audience to audience. A profitable way to
study a tragedy is to explore the theatrical potential of its
text at a few significant moments of the action by whatever means possible. This does more than offer narrow
keyhole views: a series of doors will be opened through
which readers can enter in imagination and see the play
in performance from their own perspectives. Then it
should be possible to relate these single moments to the
ongoing action and so proceed to consider the unfolding
of the narrative, which is the one element that remains
the same in all performances of a Shakespeare tragedy.

* * *

What is seen and heard is bound to change in innumerable small ways from one occasion to another, many of them highly significant, but the sequence of events on stage remains constant. Unless the text has been severely cut or altered, the narrative will always take one predetermined course, involving the same principal figures in the same sequence of entries, exits, and encounters. However differently the persons of the play have been cast and their parts acted, they are always seen in the same incidents in the same order, realigning their relationships to each other in very basic and unavoidable ways as they respond to what is happening and what is said. Elizabethan playwrights and theatre managers used to identify a play by what they called its 'plot', which was their word for this fundamental element. They would buy and sell the plots of plays before any dialogue was written.[2] A later version of the plot – we might call it an outline of stage action – was retained back-stage so that performances could be managed according to the play's defining and permanent element. Although these manuscript outlines were likely to be damaged by regular use, a number of them have survived to the present day.

It follows that a good way of studying one of Shakespeare's tragedies is to follow its plot and work out what happens on stage, moment by moment, as if following the course of a battle on a map or preparing to re-enact a crime in its original location. Drawing a number of outlines of a stage-space and marking on them a position for each person, scene by scene, is one way to discover the changing actions required by the plot. Arrows can be added to indicate successive movements and groupings. Better than that, with a single outline of a stage, chessmen, miscellaneous small coins, or toy soldiers can be used to represent the various persons of the play. While reading the dialogue and stage directions aloud, appropriate figures can then be brought onto the stage when directed to enter, and physically moved around as the dialogue dictates. Although live actors are not present and many puzzling decisions will have to be made, the play begins to be substantial in the mind's eye, and a reader's imagination becomes more adventurous and closer to the experience of actors and their audiences. Without trying to explore a text in this way, it is hard to believe how much this form of study is able to reveal about Shakespeare's plays. The process of seeking out and envisaging the actions on stage – and in some measure sharing in them – draws a close scrutiny of the text itself in order to discover the physical implications of the dialogue and the changing relationships between speakers. Speech is the spring for action in the performance of Shakespeare's plays and that action is part of what words achieve when spoken by actors on stage. This form of study awakens a reader's senses to see and to hear. It also ensures that all is viewed in the continuous sequence that is a constant in all performances. Such a process is closer to a theatrical experience than purely verbal study can ever be.

For an example that is manageably small in scope, a study of the 'plot' for the first few scenes of Act V of *Macbeth* can further illuminate moments already considered in this chapter, by establishing the context in which Shakespeare had Macbeth react to his wife's death and the means by which he draws an audience towards the tragedy's last moments so that it makes its own judgement on the entire performance. The commentary that follows moves slowly in order to show many of the choices open to actors as well as what is constant in all performances.

* * *

At the start of Act V, two persons who have not been seen before come on stage and talk together in the dark. In a performance at the original Globe Theatre the atmosphere of the scene would not have been helped by a change in lighting,[3] but the two watchful presences – one male, one female, and both unsure of themselves – are in marked contrast to the assured group that has just left the stage at the end of the previous scene, in 'manly' readiness prepared for hand-to-hand fighting (IV.iii.235–7). The dialogue is no longer in verse but in careful and mostly short-phrased prose. The first anonymous speaker has the authority of a physician but, unlike the doctor seen briefly in the previous scene, he is ill at ease and unfamiliar with his surroundings. The second speaker has a female voice and knows what Macbeth and his Lady have been doing; she may have taken a subservient and wordless role in earlier scenes. Her reply to the Doctor's question is detailed but, when asked what the sleepwalker has said, she refuses to share her knowledge. At this apprehensive moment in the duologue, Lady Macbeth enters alone, in self-absorbed silence and carrying a light. Earlier in the play she will have been greeted with every possible sign of respect but now she is discussed objectively, as someone incapable of hearing and an object of wonder, fear, and perhaps pity. What is unmistakable and, at first, unexplained is Lady Macbeth's open, sightless eyes and, soon, a repeated rubbing of her hands as if she were washing them. This introduction will encourage members of a theatre audience to watch closely and listen for the slightest sound she might make. After being carried forward by dialogue, argument and soliloquy that has often been highly charged, the play's action now entirely depends on a single person wrapped up in sleep and silence, making a few useless and repetitive gestures.

The actor is given very little help, having no one to confront or to take the light from her hands before she rubs them, and hearing no speech to which she can reply. Everything must depend on the actor's imagination, which at first finds its expression only in physical presence, upright or bent, but able to move without hindrance anywhere on stage. When thoughts are eventually expressed in words, speech comes by fits and starts, short-phrased and varied in feeling and subject matter, the connection between one utterance and another often unspoken. Lady Macbeth speaks about herself and about others, and sometimes addresses her husband as if he were present. She also seems to address some court of appeal, possibly the audience or, perhaps, another part of her own consciousness. Repetitions, exclamations, silences, and much nervous physical activity ensure that her behaviour is unprecedented in the play. Only when Lady Macbeth had first entered to read her husband's letter, and when the Porter answered the summons at the castle's gate and spoke about hell (I.v.1–14 and II.iii.1–41), did Shakespeare previously dispense with the forward impetus and control of iambic verse, as he has for almost the whole of this scene. Nowhere else is an actor so free to speak each word with whatever emphasis and whatever timing seems right at the moment. How soon, for example, is 'why then 'tis time to do't' followed by 'Hell is murky', and what impulses account for that transition and then for moving on to the following 'Fie, my lord, fie! a soldier, and afeard'?

When Lady Macbeth speaks of the 'smell of the blood' and then declares that 'All the perfumes of Arabia will not sweeten this little hand', her sensitivity seems to be heightened as her mind reaches far beyond her present situation before fixing on her own 'little' hand that is in need of cleansing. An audience's intent and questioning attention will only be partly released with her inarticulate 'Oh, oh, oh!' (l. 50). Individual spectators are left to use their imaginations and make what sense they can. The on-stage observers guide but do not define their response:

DOCTOR   What a sigh is there! The heart is sorely charg'd.
GENTLEWOMAN   I would not have such a heart in my
   bosom for the dignity of the whole body.
DOCTOR   Well, well, well.
GENTLEWOMAN   Pray God it be, sir.
DOCTOR   This disease is beyond my practice. Yet I
   have known those which have walk'd in their sleep
   who have died holily in their beds.

These words make comprehensible sense of incomprehensible suffering and, in conclusion, hint that this person is close to a troubled death. The Doctor speaks in a riddle, as if more direct comment would be too insensitive or too dangerous.

As well as responding to the present moment, audiences are encouraged to think back to earlier events when these are briefly and vividly recalled in words: the sight of blood-stained hands in need of cleansing; the pressure of time and darkness, and the need for courage; an 'old man' and the spilling of blood; the sudden murder of the Thane of Fife's wife; Macbeth's fearful 'starting', which had been likely to 'mar all'. A slow, fragmented and inescapable re-run of the play's action is shattering the peace of one of its chief agents. The past is most clearly recalled and accentuated by a sequence of repetitions immediately before Lady Macbeth leaves the stage:

> LADY MACBETH   Wash your hands, put on your night-
> gown, look not so pale. I tell you yet again,
> Banquo's buried; he cannot come out on 's grave.
> DOCTOR   Even so?
> LADY MACBETH   To bed, to bed; there's knocking at the
> gate. Come, come, come, come, give me your hand.
> What's done cannot be undone. To bed, to bed, to
> bed.

There can be no mistaking that Lady Macbeth recalls times past but her words do not explain why she should now call her husband to bed so repeatedly: that final impulse is left to the performer to imagine and express. Does the reiteration show an escalating fear and therefore a growing dependence on the reassuring presence of her husband? Or do these words, calling for his presence, acknowledge the love she had shared as his 'dearest partner of greatness' and 'dearest chuck' (I.v.13–14 and III.ii.45)? Might the wife's sexual dominance assert itself here or does an unsatisfied sexual craving surface into words? Or do these last repetitions show Lady Macbeth's practicality and strength of will, rather than betray any feeling for her 'lord' (l. 36)? Might she be sufficiently in command of herself to stop and pick up the light she had brought on stage or is this stage property ignored as if no longer effective or necessary as a means of reassurance? What the plotting of this scene ensures is that each member of the audience is left to imagine and piece together from many fragments what Lady Macbeth feels as she leaves the stage for what will prove to be the last time. To different degrees, they have been led to think and feel with her, experiencing her pain and distress. The Doctor supplies only a sense of foreboding, a recourse to conventional religion, and a fearful refusal to say all that he thinks.

This presentation of an isolated figure, in a way that draws the closest attention and yet will puzzle an audience and is beyond the understanding of informed onlookers, has no precedent in the play or, indeed, in any other play by Shakespeare. The action stands still, suspended in a dream-like hiatus and needing a clear change of direction in order to continue. That is provided by the sound of drums and then the entry of banners and soldiers, heralding a new scene located at some distance from Macbeth's castle. At its centre a series of purposeful, unambiguous speeches in strongly marked but not always regular iambics give an account of the besieged Macbeth, who is now either mad or possessed by 'valiant fury'. Reported facts and evocative images now leave little room for uncertainty:

> CAITHNESS ... for certain
> He cannot buckle his distemper'd cause
> Within the belt of rule.
> ANGUS Now does he feel
> His secret murders sticking on his hands;
> Now minutely revolts upbraid his faith-breach;
> Those he commands move only in command,
> Nothing in love. Now does he feel his title
> Hang loose about him, like a giant's robe.
> (V.ii.13–21)

Six of the scene's ten speeches start half way through an iambic line, implying that the four leaders are listening

intently to each other and probably standing close together. An audience will see the nucleus of a new and
armed force that seeks retribution: Caithness and
Mentieth enter the play for the first time, unnamed in
the dialogue; Angus has been with Duncan but previously
has said very little; Lennox, also present, was last seen accompanying Macbeth. Before they all march off, Lennox
foresees that blood will be spilt to 'dew the sovereign
flower and drown the weeds'. Briefly but unmistakably he
invites the audience to view a mysterious or spiritual
process as well as the political and moral issues that are
verbally explicit and implicit in the stage action. On the
eve of battle, this soldier might recall to the minds of an
audience the earlier references in the play to 'heaven's
cherubin', 'God's benison', and a 'healing benediction'
(I.vii.22; II.iv.40; and IV.iii.156). As he speaks, the focus of
attention is wide and the issues raised by the plot of the
play are at their most comprehensive.

After only thirty-one lines, the action shifts back to
Macbeth's castle and speech becomes both freer and
more demanding on actor and audience. Emphatically
dismissing those bringing news of thanes deserting to the
enemy, Macbeth enters with the now-silent Doctor and
other nameless, silent attendants. 'Bring me no more
reports; let them fly all' are his first words and then, as
the Witches had prophesied, he lays claim to 'security':

> The mind I sway by and the heart I bear
> Shall never sag with doubt nor shake with fear.
>
> (V.iii.9–10)

Does he say this because he truly *is* unafraid or because
he recognizes the seeds of weakness within himself? The
text does not tell us but at the very next moment any
semblance of calm evaporates. Shakespeare has so manip-
ulated the on-stage action that, against Macbeth's orders,
a further messenger enters who is terrified by the news
he brings of an approaching 'English force' ten thousand
soldiers strong. With 'Death of thy soul', the 'boy' is
ordered away, Macbeth admitting that 'Those linen

cheeks of thine / Are counsellors to fear' (ll.16–17). This unexpected entry has triggered the first in a sequence of huge transitions in mood and subject matter. Not only does Macbeth feel a sudden eruption of fear, but also a pressing need for Seyton, an attendant neither seen nor mentioned before, who will respond to orders until very near the end. When Seyton does not immediately enter, some unspoken impulse leads Macbeth to survey his entire life in words so packed with physical detail, political awareness, and sensuous evocation that, as in the sleep-walking scene, forward action is halted:

> *Seyton!* – I am sick at heart,
> When I behold – *Seyton*, I say! – This push
> Will cheer me ever, or disseat me now.
> I have liv'd long enough. My way of life
> Is fall'n into the sear, the yellow leaf;
> And that which should accompany old age,
> As honour, love, obedience, troops of friends,
> I must not look to have; but, in their stead,
> Curses not loud but deep, mouth-honour, breath,
> Which the poor heart would fain deny, and dare not.
> *Seyton!*
> SEYTON What's your gracious pleasure?
> (ll.19–29; *italics added*)

Stage-time has been extended far beyond the present moment and the location might momentarily be anywhere. No one on stage has words with which to respond as Macbeth acknowledges that the wished-for consequences of wearing the golden crown will never be his. The image of a dying leaf and the eddying rhythm of his words ensure a stillness in which the sensation of loss is finely expressed at the very moment in which it is experienced.

When we read the text of this scene, each transition is over in an instant and, because Macbeth moves so completely from one state of mind to another, we may not sense the inevitable physical manifestations. In performance, however, Shakespeare would expect an audience to see an actor's 'whole function suiting / With forms to his conceit', as the First Player in *Hamlet* provides example (II.ii.549–50). Feeling the sudden force of these contrary and deep-set feelings can be like being close to a great timber beam as it withstands a mighty storm and is struck repeatedly by lightning so that it is about to split and shatter the entire building. Much that Macbeth says seems to be wrung from him involuntarily, revealing thoughts and feelings he has not spoken of before. When he breaks off, not saying what he 'beholds', his thought quickens with a pun on cheer/chair and then stalls, leaving the present 'now' to be caught up in what can no longer be his. He hears curses and mere words, which the speakers would 'fain deny and dare not', and then shuts these thoughts out by calling yet again for Seyton. Unlike Lady Macbeth in her sleepwalking, he gives himself over to each change with sufficient control to be aware of its consequences in loss of trust and fellowship, and in hopeless action. Whatever individual words mean or imply when they are spoken, the action here and in the remainder of the play shows Macbeth increasingly tormented, isolated, and at bay. Meantime, in alternating scenes, his opponents grow in numbers, meet little resistance, and become increasingly secure.

Shakespeare's handling of the action has ensured that an audience views an inevitable process that the hero cannot reverse, and also his increasingly lonely journey that changes direction frequently as he searches out his innermost thoughts and draws upon every reserve. At the end, both Macbeth and the actor who plays the role will be close to exhaustion, physically, emotionally, and mentally, and yet they must fight with Macduff, who is so certain in purpose that he has refused all other fighting and kept his full strength for this moment. Every word spoken in the last Act is affected by this process, which has repeatedly held the audience's closest attention and created a context in which what is not yet confronted is likely to be the most noted factor in its response; what has been lost, often present in mind. So, for example, a silence indicated by the incomplete verse-line 'She should have died hereafter', if it should follow those

words, will mark and draw attention to the transition to a
more general thought, 'There would have been a time
for such a word', and that leads Macbeth back to his own
consciousness and a view of wasted and worthless effort:

> To-morrow, and to-morrow, and to-morrow,
> Creeps in this petty pace from day to day
> To the last syllable of recorded time,
> And all our yesterdays have lighted fools
> The way to dusty death. Out, out, brief candle!
> Life's but a walking shadow, a poor player,
> That struts and frets his hour upon the stage,
> And then is heard no more; it is a tale
> Told by an idiot, full of sound and fury,
> Signifying nothing.
>
> (V.v.19–28)

Here, again, his senses seem to surge and then fall backwards, only to return again with speech concentrated into
precise images of a forgotten theatrical performance, the
extinguishing of a single candle's light, and an idiot's
words. Should the silence come before 'She should have
died hereafter', it will mark how far Macbeth has to travel
in his mind before he can hold on to the thought of his
wife's death and his own inadequacy. That he says
nothing about his suffering will not diminish the strength
of his feeling or its effectiveness in performance: physically and emotionally, Macbeth's pain is unmistakable at
this moment in the play's plot. He may choke back expression of it or look wordlessly for someone who might
offer compassion or understanding. More certainly, he
will be seen to 'pull in resolution' as he begins to realize
he must 'try the last' alone (V.v.42 and V.viii.32).

As we have already noticed, Malcolm has total
command over what he is saying in the tragedy's final
speech. His quick movements of thought, after so much
seems to have been dredged out of the protagonist's consciousness; his assured stance at the head of the troops,
after his opponent's varied entries and exits; his ready acceptance of the fruits of victory, after young Siward and

Macduff have engaged in mortal combat, and not himself: all this, experienced in one concerted process, creates a scene in which an audience's attention must also change, as if with a sudden and crashed change of gear. Some spectators may take everything at its new face-value, consigning Macbeth and his Lady to execration as 'this dead butcher, and his fiend-like queen' (V.viii.69), but the plotting of the last Act of the tragedy will ensure that others will respond less certainly. Although they are not told how to evaluate it, they will not forget Macbeth's determination to 'die with harness on [his] back' (V.v.52) at the time when he knew defeat to be inevitable:

> I will not yield,
> To kiss the ground before young Malcolm's feet
> And to be baited with the rabble's curse,
> Though Birnam wood be come to Dunsinane,
> And thou oppos'd, being of no woman born,
> Yet I will try the last. Before my body
> I throw my warlike shield. Lay on, Macduff;
> And damn'd be him that first cries 'Hold, enough!'
>   (V.viii.27–34).

The experience of being present during the performance of the entire play will still, in some measure, register in their unconscious minds and, perhaps, in their conscious minds as well. At the end of the play, when the dismembered and bloody head is brought on stage, members of an audience may remember and reflect upon those images of peace, honour, love and trust that had animated that face only a few minutes earlier. All this is more likely to register in real time as the audience leaves the theatre with the compounded experiences of a performance still living in their minds.

* * *

A study of the themes and stories of Shakespeare's tragedies will not sufficiently account for what they achieve in performance. Macbeth's ambition, sense of honour, and military prowess, his relationship to his wife, and their shared responsibility for the crimes committed in achieving the crown, lead to the corruption of two greatly gifted persons but how they are experienced by an audience depends on how they have been presented on stage. The witches' supernatural powers, the structures of society in early Jacobean England, and the ideas then current about kingship, religion, and human consciousness, together with social and family relations, are major themes raised by the play, both on the page and in performance, but an investigation of all this will not lead to an understanding of an audience's experience of the play in a theatre. That depends on what Shakespeare's fellow professionals called the plotting of the tragedy: how the focus of attention changes, bringing forward new elements or developing what has been seen before, satisfying expectation or failing to do so, taking a wide or a narrow view of what happens on stage, or the focus of attention settling nowhere for very long. The audience is alternately fed with information and left to search for explanation: like a horse in harness or a guest at a great banquet, it is sometimes given little option and sometimes encouraged to proceed and feed as it chooses.

When we look at a landscape or a painting, or when we enter someone else's living room, we are never aware of everything that is before our eyes, only of what we are looking for or what catches our attention by reason of its dominant position or its contrast with everything in its vicinity, or because it is unexpected or newly introduced into the context. Much the same considerations apply when we see one of Shakespeare's plays in performance, except that these processes are not left to chance. The nature of our experience is, then, controlled by how the author has ordered the play's action and the manner of its presentation. A study of Shakespeare's skill in plotting will bring us closer to what the plays achieve in performance and to the changing nature of his art.

How the action of each tragedy is uniquely shaped is especially evident in their final Acts. After preparatory

exchanges in duologue, the large-scale final scene of
Hamlet brings the entire company of actors on stage. An
'incensed' duel just before its end (V.ii.293) draws an
intense focus that is then widened by sustained speeches
and new arrivals. In *Othello,* an intimate focus on
Desdemona and Emilia alone together is followed by a
busy and confused street-scene that in turn yields to a
slowly unwinding bedroom-scene with only a few persons
present, and one prolonged and several rapid killings.
The conclusion is more formal, with one long and crucial
speech and the stage crowded with onlookers. For the last
Act of *King Lear,* as the end of its twin narratives slowly
unfolds, the protagonist is only on stage intermittently, at
first a prisoner but confident in Cordelia's love, and then
entering, many lines later, carrying her dead body, so torn
between hope and despair that before he dies it seems
that 'He knows not what he says' (V.iii.293). Action
throughout the two last tragedies moves from one group
of persons to another and one country to another until
their final scenes. Then, exiled from Rome, Coriolanus is
suddenly assassinated by nameless conspirators who allow
him no time for words. In contrast, royally attired and attended, Cleopatra kills herself in her 'monument' and accounts for her own actions in sustained and lavishly
imagistic speech. Early in the sequence of tragedies, the
death of Titus Andronicus is one among many others that
happen in quick succession; it is followed by the handing
out of judgements and punishments. In contrast, Romeo
speaks many words before killing himself and Juliet very
few, and then a long sequence of enquiries and confes-
sions follow, presided over by the Prince. The variety of
presentation is obvious, even in these very brief accounts,
and each of these conclusions is the result of choices that
Shakespeare made with only the slightest guidance from
his narrative sources. The plotting of each tragedy merits
careful attention as it modifies the experience of an
audience and the final effect of performance.

* * *

While the finer details of Shakespeare's 'plotting' are more readily discovered in rehearsals or numerous visits to a theatre, its basic strategy can be studied in the play-text. Attention should be paid to those moments when the dialogue indicates a clear shift of consciousness for its leading persons. For example, as the last Act of *Macbeth* has shown, the entrance of someone from elsewhere bringing new information or reporting a change of fortune will often produce a new perspective on the action and so reveal thoughts and feelings not previously expressed, as if they have been hidden or are still, even now, not fully conscious. But a plot can also manipulate how an audience reacts. Events that are wholly unexpected and unheralded are the most potent means of doing this, even when no one on stage greets them with an expression of surprise. Indeed, when that happens, the effect is often all the stronger because the audience will respond instinctively and in its own way. When asked the title of the play that is about to be performed, Hamlet calls it '*The Mousetrap*', as if he expects the audience to be caught by its unexpected action. It proves to be a fitting name because, in the event, the performance does 'unkennel' the secret guilt of Claudius (III.ii.79) and his own feelings take over from those of the enacted drama. *The Tragedy of Hamlet* is itself full of unexpected turns in the action that can, similarly, provoke spectators to enter imaginatively into the drama and draw upon their own life-experiences.

By the end of the fourth Act, the audience knows that Ophelia has died, as many may have expected, but when the play was first performed the appearance of two clowns at the top of the next scene, in the roles of a gravedigger and his assistant, must have been a stunning surprise. No such persons have appeared in the play before, and except for some tongue-tied 'seafaring men' and a foreign army halting during a march, everyone else either belongs to the Court at Elsinore or has arrived there on an official visit. Nor have death and suicide been used previously as topics about which to make jokes. Later, when the principal clown is joined by Hamlet and

Horatio, satirical comment on lawyers, politicians, courtiers, and buyers of land are also unprecedented. Hamlet's opinion that 'the toe of the peasant comes so near the heel of the courtier, he galls his kibe' (V.i.134–5) is also surprising because nothing seen or heard in the play has given evidence of this. Hamlet's affectionate recollection of Yorick, the clown, recalls a part of his past not mentioned before and brings a sudden physical awkwardness as his 'gorge rises' at the sight of this particular skull. That both he and the Gravedigger had known Yorick some twenty years previously and that this person talking with Hamlet had started digging graves the 'very day that young Hamlet was born' (ll. 143–4) are two unlikely coincidences, the more remarkable in that the clown acts as if unaware to whom he is speaking. Spectators will react in different ways to this scene: those who laugh will find that dramatic tension slackens and their own reactions to the inequalities and burdens of everyday life start to surface; those who do not laugh may become impatient or sense that Hamlet is drawing near to his own death. Some who start by laughing will grow increasingly apprehensive, beginning to find everything momentous.

Another sudden change of focus and idiom is introduced with the entry of Osric near the start of the next and final scene. This young courtier seems to belong to another more comedic and fanciful play but, from what has been said and done earlier, many in the audience will at once realize that he brings a treacherous proposal from the king. His first words provoke Hamlet to speak aside and fiercely condemn him for possession of a large and fertile estate, adding that it is 'a vice to know him' (V.ii.86). Not until Osric has gone, does he give an explanation:

> OSRIC   I commend my duty to your lordship.
> HAMLET   Yours, yours. [*Exit* Osric.] He does well to commend it himself; there are no tongues else for's turn.
> HORATIO   This lapwing runs away with the shell on his head.

HAMLET   'A did comply, sir, with his dug before 'a
suck'd it. Thus has he, and many more of the same
bevy, that I know the drossy age dotes on, only got
the tune of the time and outward habit of encounter – a kind of yesty collection, which carries
them through and through the most fann'd and
winnowed opinions; and do but blow them to their
trial, the bubbles are out.

(ll. 176–88)

These packed lines of allusive and abusive prose are
usually cut from present-day productions but they stand
in the texts of both the 'good' Second Quarto and the
revised First Folio, even though neither compositor was
able to make total sense of them.

For Shakespeare's contemporaries, as the narrative is
obviously approaching its conclusion, the entrance of two
clowns and then a strangely laughable courtier will have
brought performance rather closer to contemporary
reality and awakened a sense of daily injustice and
comedy. At a crucial juncture near the start of the play
Hamlet had pronounced 'the time' to be 'out of joint'
and acknowledged his duty to 'set it right' (I.v.189–90)
and now, near its close, Shakespeare has prompted the audience to conflate that dramatic 'time' with actual time by
introducing three new roles that call for highly individual
and ostensibly theatrical performances. Before dramatic
focus concentrates on the final outcome of the action, the
persons of the play, the actors who perform them, and
members of the audience – all three parties in any theatrical event – are called upon to respond individually as the
tragic story merges with events of their off-stage lives.[4] In
present-day performances the contrasting physical presence of each new person in the play is likely to make a
stronger impression than their detailed verbal accounts of
off-stage realities. As if Shakespeare knew that the words
would quickly date, the dialogue insists on the physical
business of digging bones out of a grave and flourishing a
hat in order to keep cool: the games that clowns and
comedy actors can play with such stage properties do not

date, and help to establish an audience's different involvement with the action.

Just before the end of the play, after Osric has taken charge of the duel to ensure its murderous intent and when, with 'purposes mistook' (l. 376), the King, Queen, and Laertes all lie dead and Hamlet is mortally wounded, Shakespeare called unexpectedly for the off-stage sounds of marching and cannon-shot. Surprisingly, Osric knows what has happened and announces the entry of Fortinbras at the head of his victorious army. More surprises follow when Hamlet gives his 'dying voice' to the election of this foreign prince as the next King of Denmark, and some English Ambassadors make a first entry to the play. Almost at once, Fortinbras orders four of his captains to bear the dead Hamlet 'like a soldier' to another 'stage', accompanied by more cannon-shot. Fortinbras says little directly or comprehensively about the outcome of the tragedy, only that Hamlet would have proved 'most royal' had he lived and 'been put on' – which is to say, pompously and somewhat ambiguously, that had he lived he would have been a fitting king for Denmark (ll. 389–90). What happens physically on stage is more likely to shape the audience's reaction, both action and sound being now more eloquent and less equivocal than words.

Horatio has promised to tell 'how these things came about' but Shakespeare did not write that speech, giving in its place a general account of events that the audience already knows well enough:

> So shall you hear
> Of carnal, bloody, and unnatural acts;
> Of accidental judgments, casual slaughters;
> Of deaths put on by cunning and forc'd cause;
> And, in this upshot, purposes mistook
> Fall'n on th' inventors' heads – all this can I
> Truly deliver.
>
> (ll. 371–7)

This falls far short of reporting Hamlet and his cause 'aright'. In effect, much that might be thought the author's and the actors' task is passed to members of the audience as, individually and corporately, they respond to the entire performance. In so far as they have lived with its action, they will make the play their own and draw their own conclusions.

Shakespeare was invariably and unpredictably inventive in shaping the concluding scenes of the tragedies. For example, Gratiano, Desdemona's uncle, makes an unexpected first entrance in the last Act of *Othello* and still later, after the audience has been told that he has 'no weapon' (V.ii.259), Othello takes a third that must be found on stage, and with that kills himself. The eventual death of Othello is over in a moment, before any of the onlookers can prevent this last unexpected action. Comment is brief and uninformative;

> LODOVICO   O bloody period!
> GRATIANO   All that is spoke is marr'd.
>   ...
> CASSIO   This did I fear, but thought he had no weapon;
>   For he was great of heart.
>
> (ll. 360–4)

With the tragedy's concluding speech, Lodovico draws attention to Iago, blaming him for the 'tragic loading of this bed' and ordering the dead bodies to be hid as an object that 'poisons sight'. He then gives instructions for dealing with Othello's possessions, before turning briefly to the 'censure' of Iago, 'this hellish villain', and to affairs of state. In no other tragedy did Shakespeare hide the dead bodies before the play ends. Several times the plotting of this last Act is likely to shock and frustrate an audience, leaving them with a sense of helplessness as well as feelings of pity and awe.

Among many surprises in the last scene of *King Lear* are Edmund's one 'good' deed, which fails to save Cordelia's life, and the last desperate actions of Lear's other two daughters. Perhaps most unexpected of all in early performances would have been the death of Cordelia. Anyone in the audience who had read about the historical King Lear would expect her to remain alive, and the majority, not knowing the story, might believe that she will until very near the end, as Lear does when he acts and speaks several times as if she were still living. At the end this tragic hero speaks only a few very simple words as he struggles to breathe, which ensures that the audience, like everyone on stage, will pay close attention. The text of the First Folio concludes the play with the stage direction, '*Exeunt with a dead march*', which would bring the tragedy to a slow and verbally silent ending as the dead bodies are lifted up and carried away. This would give an audience time in which to reflect on what has happened and be drawn to share in what is called a 'general woe' and the 'weight of this sad time' (V.iii.319, 323).

In the fifth Act of *Macbeth*, as the plotting concentrates attention on the innermost thoughts and instinctive feelings of the two protagonists, and the Thanes desert Macbeth, other persons enter for the first time to hold attention on their own account, and fresh information complicates an audience's view of the action. Some of these interventions provide a contrast with Macbeth's state of mind: for example, the cool professionalism of the English general, Siward, compared with Macbeth's physical energy and ruthlessness, which have earned him the name of 'Bellona's bridegroom' (I.ii.55). The 'unshrinking' courage of young Siward in single combat (V.viii.42) contrasts moments later with Macbeth's initial refusal to fight Macduff, the one person the Witches warned that he should fear. For early audiences, the biggest surprise would probably have been Macduff's declaration that he was 'from his mother's womb / Untimely ripp'd' (V.viii.15–16); this information, not even alluded to before, reveals at the very last moment how the Witches' prophecy that 'none of woman born / Shall harm Macbeth' (IV.i.80–1) will not protect him against this adversary's revenge for the murder of his defenceless wife and little children. Realizing how this prophecy will be fulfilled, together with the sight of soldiers screening their numbers by bearing green boughs cut from

Birnham Wood, will send an audience's thoughts back to the Witches, perhaps as far as the first short scene, in which they agree to meet with Macbeth upon the heath. When Malcolm is hailed as King of Scotland the audience may remember that Macbeth's off-stage death was the conclusion of his committal to 'the imperial theme' (I.iii.128–9) regardless of the consequences. The exact nature of the Witches' power has still not been explained, but in the last scenes an audience is prompted to consider, as best they can, whether Macbeth could ever have renounced his determination to win the crown.

The plot of this tragedy had given earlier clues, but no more than that. When Macbeth interrogates two anonymous candidates before hiring them to murder Banquo, both declare themselves in no need of persuasion but already so incensed by 'the vile blows and buffets of the world' that they are 'reckless what / [they] do to spite the world' (III.i.97–113). By continuing to persuade these 'best of cutthroats' (III.iv.16) whose 'spirits shine through' them (III.i.127), Macbeth reveals the extent of his own moral insecurity. The lengthy and largely static episode in which Malcolm, suspecting Macduff's motives for arriving in England, gives himself the attributes of an 'untitled tyrant bloody-sceptr'ed' (IV.iii.104), provides the audience with a verbal picture of the motives of a tyrant and the political and social consequences of Macbeth's regicide. Macduff's few words and troubled silences in reply demonstrate how such a tyrant's power keeps criticism muted until its cruelty is no longer supportable. In the last scenes, the dramatic focus is widened by less verbal means and in a more mysterious direction. Seyton, who answers Macbeth's calls, arms him for the final battle and brings him necessary information, has been given no clear status or relationship to his master and no suggestion of an independent life so that his very presence, in his late entry to the play, can seem fated or inevitable, like so much else as the action draws to its close. He does, however, answer to a name that, when spoken, is so similar to *Satan* that it can sound identical, a coincidence of Shakespeare's contrivance that may have prompted some in the play's original audiences to think that the devil himself had come to claim Macbeth as his own.

When writing a tragedy Shakespeare did not set out to present a conflict between the forces or representatives of abstract ideas, such as good and evil, love and honour, fate and free will, or authority and barbarism, and bring the opposites to a final reckoning. His concern was to present a narrative ending in the death of its titular hero or heroes while progressively developing and deepening the audience's perception of what is happening. The texts are evidence of a continual experiment to devise ways of achieving these ends, alternately increasing and reducing the numbers and variety of persons in the casts, the length and scope of narratives, the relative importance of speech and spectacle. Sometimes the working of fate is a dominant impression – a destiny that shapes our ends, a fate written in the stars, an ancient magic woven into a handkerchief – and sometimes self-determination defies fate, as intellect or instinct controls the action. What Lear imagines to be true, how Macbeth dies, why Othello kills and then kisses Desdemona, are crucial issues and yet, even here, the audience's reception is a vital component of the theatrical event since nothing that is spoken gives a clear and comprehensive judgement on what happens. It seems as if everything in these plays has been calculated to ensure that members of an audience live imaginatively with the dramatic action as the inner nature of its principal persons and the consequences of their actions are progressively revealed. Each of Shakespeare's tragedies presents a fearful and seemingly inevitable action, so that it awakens in members of its audience an imaginative response that draws upon the experiences of their own lives and their own world.

Towards the end of the series of tragedies that covered almost the whole of Shakespeare's creative life, two changes were introduced. In the last two, *Coriolanus* and *Antony and Cleopatra*, the central persons are further removed from the audience: there are fewer soliloquies and asides, choices are made without sharing the process by which they are reached, the number of other persons is larger than previously, the language handled more tightly, with less impression of thoughts gathering assurance or surprising the speaker. In consequence the audience's view will be less concentrated and a whole way of life will seem to be at issue rather than the fortunes of hero or heroine, despite their extraordinary abilities and dominant status. The audience's experience is likely to be more concurring than before, less partisan and committed to hero or heroine. The other clear development in Shakespeare's writing was the growing trust that he placed in the actors, giving them both more freedom and more responsibility. This becomes evident from *Hamlet* onwards, as the following chapter will argue – his reliance on actors continuing to increase through all the later plays, comedies as well as tragedies.

* * *

The handling of narrative should be a primary concern when studying the text of any of Shakespeare's plays. Elizabethans called this 'the plot' and it was the means by which the playwright could control the response of audiences and influence their experience of the play. It is constant in effect, from one production of a play to another and from one performance to another, and its influence is wide, since the effect of every word is liable to depend on what the audience knows and expects when it is spoken. An incident that comes as a surprise receives an attention different from that given to one that delays forward interest or resolves differences and conflicts. In tragedies, the inclusion of persons with little connection to the protagonist, and verbal references to events outside the immediate context of the story, are devices that alter the perspective in which the main events are viewed, and consequently, the audience's engagement with the tragic action. To study one of these plays as they would be experienced in performance, the course of its narrative must be closely followed and attention paid to the changes this brings about in an audience's responses. This process will be slow but also rewarding because in this way a play can come alive, moment by moment, in a reader's imagination.

Notes

1. This moment is illustrated in Laurence Olivier, *On Acting* (London and New York: Weidenfeld and Nicolson, 1986), p. 328.
2. See, for example, Andrew Gurr, *The Shakespearian Playing Companies* (Oxford: Clarendon Press, 1996), p. 102.
3. During a winter's afternoon, however, the entire theatre is likely to have grown darker towards the end of a performance as the sun was progressively setting.
4. The clown who played the Gravedigger originally, and for whom the role could have been written, was almost certainly Robert Armin, who also created the role of Touchstone and stamped that part with his own *persona*; see Chapter 1, pp. 15–16, above.

3

Annotating Silence: Speechless Eloquence[1]

On the pages of a book, Shakespeare's words say everything for a reader and can arouse endless reactions, associations, and visual images. But his playscripts were written to do more than that. In theatrical performance, with the help of actors and their many supporters, they take on a living presence and a spectator views a complex phenomenon, a re-making of the everyday world that transforms ordinary events and can transcend or intensify ordinary experiences. The words are still there but as part of an event in which they have meanings that a reader might never consider and, indeed, might judge to be impossible or plain wrong. Words are eaten up in performance and digested, with much added, subtracted, accentuated, or ignored. They give rise to a happening on stage that on every occasion is unique and, to some degree, surprising.

The contrast between a play read and a play experienced has increasingly occupied editors of Shakespeare's texts. They now take as much care with stage directions as they do with dialogue and their annotations provide a useful index of current practices in the theatrical study of Shakespeare. Space is sometimes found for footnotes describing how individual performers have spoken certain words or accentuated specific meanings by intonation, timing, or emphasis. They also report how words have been supplemented by gesture or stage business. Information drawn from stage-histories, photographs, drawings or paintings and extensive quotations from reviews or personal recollections are used to place the edition's reader as far as possible in a similar relationship to the text as a member of an audience viewing a performance.

Unfortunately, this task is more easily contemplated than achieved and it can never be complete, since no one could notice everything that happened on stage in one particular moment of a performance. Details of movement, intonation, and embodiment are infinite in number and difficult to describe; and any effect is fleeting. Editors will sometimes quote expressive eye-witness accounts of key moments but this involves ruthless selection from a great many testimonies and usually makes no reference to an incident's place in a whole production. Journalistic reviews seldom pay attention to the wider cultural or theatrical context of a performance or give an account of the critic's personal prejudices. Some editors prefer to describe moments in a hypothetical staging that they conjecture from a study of the text and Elizabethan stage conditions, even though the result of such speculation is more like a diagram or map than a view of a play coming to life in a theatre. All these modes of annotation take a reader some way towards a play in performance but only in fragmentary and abbreviated form. At best, they are concerned with what can happen to certain speeches and words, rather than a play's physical and interactive embodiment of a text or the effects of narrative and dramatic structure on both performers and audience.

* * *

An editor who wishes to show what life a text has in performance sets out on a task that can never be complete. The difficulties may best be illustrated when words are at their simplest, and an actor's performance is necessarily the principal means of holding attention and engaging the imagination of an audience. It will not be sufficient to describe how the uncomplicated words have been or could be spoken, or to note any gestures that have been used: an actor's state of mind and body – the exact nature of an actual presence – will also affect the audience. An editor would have to recount how the accumulated experience of the entire play until this moment influences both the actor's performance and the audience's response.

When Richard the Third's last speech repeats his earlier 'A horse! A horse! My kingdom for a horse!' (*Richard III*, V.iv.7 and 13) a reader will easily understand the words without grasping what is happening on stage. What gestures, timing, or inflection does the actor use and how are the two repeated monosyllables varied for each occasion? Since the first time he spoke the exact same words at the beginning of the short scene, has he become more desperate or more confident, weary, or energized, more deranged and disfigured or more self-controlled and self-aware? In what way are the repeated words in this speech the culmination of earlier expressions of need and intention? Having spoken the words for this second time, does Richard leave the stage to seek his own death, or to kill Richmond? How does this speech prepare him for the fight in the next scene, which must provide the conclusion of his performance? An editor faces huge difficulties in attempting to annotate Richard's final moments because the impression made by this tragic hero is not defined by words. Not only are the preceding words capable of very different implications but the actor's physical bearing at the end of his long role must also be taken into account.

Antony Hammond, the Arden Shakespeare's latest editor, discusses the sources of Richard's last words but neither the reason for their repetition nor any meaning or effect they might have. With regard to the fight, he notes its importance and identifies a textual problem:

> This, the most physically exciting moment in the play, is badly served by the [Quarto's] stage-directions. The minimum to make it actable has been added here, but

the director ought to feel free to improvise to make this wordless encounter between Good and Evil as symbolically effective as possible.

While recognizing the physical nature of the fight, the editor assumes, without discussion, that it has a single moral effect. Several paintings and many photographs, together with verbal accounts of performance, show other dramatic possibilities than those considered here – expressions of courage, endurance, defiance, or, even, triumph, expressed in an actor's very stance and individual features. Performance will always be more complicated than the depersonalized moral message described in this annotation.

With less space for comment in the much earlier New Penguin edition (1969), E. A. J. Honigmann lets the cries for a horse pass without comment but he also stresses the importance of the wordless encounter and provides the same moral interpretation while offering his own instruction to both director and actor:

> This duel, in which Good overcomes Evil, is the play's supreme confrontation. It passes without a word, perhaps to emphasize its symbolic and ritual implications. Richard should be given all the violent physical action, and Richmond must bear himself calmly, with complete self-assurance.

Again, no alternative effect or actual performance is considered but the editor's 'perhaps' alerts his reader to uncertainties in this climactic confrontation and the personal exposure it ensures.

John Jowett's annotations in the more recent Oxford edition (2000) are literary and historical, rather than theatrical. They note that Richard's call for a horse is 'famous' and echoes of it 'often parodical'. Three possible sources are identified and two mutually exclusive interpretations of the words are offered: it is either a cry that the loss of a horse has lost him his kingdom or a call for a 'fresh horse to continue fighting at any cost'. Jowett notes that there is no historical authority for the single combat but that a similar ending is found in *The True Tragedy of Richard the Third* published in 1594. He adds that this fight 'has often been impressive and sustained in the theatre' but says nothing about its possible effect. Annotations in Janis Lull's 1999 Cambridge edition are even less about the play in performance. They note how the call for a horse was to become 'famous', and identify a 'similar line in *The True Tragedy*', but offer nothing about the words' meaning or the final fight.

Some verbally simple and repetitive moments are so naturally phrased that without some editorial comment a reader may not notice any difficulty of meaning or need for action. Lear's 'Never, never, never, never, never' as he sees Cordelia lying dead is obviously remarkable (V.iii.308) but a reader might benefit from being told how very differently the sequence has been spoken, whispered, or exclaimed; how hesitant or assured the actor has been. Intellectual issues are involved here, concerning fate, free will, and comprehension, and the range of possible emotions is huge, from fear to tenderness, desperation, submission, endurance, or anger. In his Introduction to the latest Arden edition, R. A. Foakes draws special attention to these words:

> one astonishing and heart-rending blank verse line brings [Lear] and the audience to face death not only as the loss of all that is worth cherishing, but as utter oblivion; there are no flights of angels to hint at some possible compensatory heaven, but only the crushing sense that a process which started with a refusal to speak more than the word 'nothing' finds its culmination in death and the bleakness of 'never'.   (p. 78)

A reader has been given a sensitive and deeply considered reaction to the simple words, which could not be contained within the customary bounds of annotation, and yet more remains to be added if the moment is to be presented as experienced in performance. What physical effect does the speaking of these words have on the speaker, and what are his feelings? Is he weeping? Does he continue to look at Cordelia or does he shut his eyes or focus attention elsewhere or into space? Does his physical strength grow or weaken with the repetitions? Does it seem that Lear has lost his way, or found it? Each different embodiment of this moment will have its own emotional charge and so modify the effect of the simple words.

The text of *King Lear* has many repetitions awaiting an actor's performance. For Lear's last speech, textual variations, the unavoidable physicality of death, and the presence of his dead daughter have given rise to lively critical debate. The New Arden's annotation notes that Lear's final lines 'complicate the ending by their very ambiguity', and from the final repetition of two simple words, 'Look there, look there!' concludes that the hero 'dies with all his attention focused on Cordelia, not any longer on himself'. What the dying Lear has seen on her lips, to whom he speaks, and why and how he repeats these few words, have to go without notice, although the dramatist's reliance on such elements of performance might be considered the most innovatory feature of this passage. At such a moment, feeling and sensation are so deeply based and powerful, the text so simple, and meaning so uncertain, that annotation can scarcely cope with a single possibility. G. K. Hunter, in the much earlier New Penguin edition (1972), keeps a tight rein on commentary. In contrast to the Arden's, his Introduction explains that Lear's 'climactic fivefold' *never* expresses his 'rejection of a world full of unimportant somethings' (p. 26). His annotation of the final words states that 'Clearly Lear imagines he sees Cordelia coming to life again', and then briefly debates whether he 'dies of joy' or in 'a mere delirium.' Hunter adds that choice between these alternatives is 'not very important for the play as a whole' and that it 'would be difficult for any actor to project a precise interpretation'. The Oxford edition published in 2000 prints a text by Gary Taylor that follows the Quarto 'when it seems defensible' (p. 84), and gives a version of Lear's final moments that is much shorter than usual but includes the final non-verbal 'O, o, o, o.' of its copy-text. Stanley Wells, who provided the annotations for this edition, comments: 'Rosenberg, pp. 319–22, records a variety of ways in which actors have portrayed Lear's death': an annotation that adds very little unless a reader has access to a library sufficiently stocked to have a copy of *The Masks of 'King Lear'* (1972). This editor either thought that the manner of this tragic death was of little consequence or found that adequate discussion of the question was impracticable. While Lear's last words can be spoken in many different ways, the actor's presence, as it has changed during the course of the play, will always sustain and shape an audience's experience of this emotionally charged and physically weak moment, leaving its members to follow closely and sense its meanings according to the set of their own minds, their imaginations, and the experience offered by the entire play in performance. What is seen and heard on stage at this moment is only a part of what influences an audience.

Perhaps an editor's main concern when annotating verbally simple but physically and emotionally significant speeches should be to indicate a range of possibilities and give some impression of how the play has been acted and received on one or two specific occasions. Or questions might be raised. For example, what happens towards the end of *Twelfth Night* in the silence before or after the incomplete verse-line of Olivia's one contribution, 'Most wonderful'? What physical sign of her feelings can be seen and how do other persons on stage react? Is it only wonder that 'enwraps' her now and is she sure that it is not 'madness' (see IV.iii.3–4)? Does the performance express pleasure or confusion? A little later, when Sebastian replies to his sister's 'My father had a mole upon his brow' with the simple words, 'And so had mine,' his actions and very presence in the silence indicated by the incomplete verse-line can say more than the words themselves about remembered intimacy or present amazement, pleasure, tenderness, confidence, or impatience (V.i.234–5). Readers can easily ignore these critical issues but, when simple words are placed so crucially, an actor's performance inevitably modifies reception of an entire play. Comedies almost invariably end with wordless moments accompanied by kisses, laughter, or dancing, or with withdrawal to some other place for celebration, and how these shared and wordless actions are performed will bring the plot's uncertainties to whatever resolution each particular enactment of the drama has achieved.[2] Carrying a different charge at the end of each performance, they bring actors and spectators together in a common acceptance of the play's conclusion, according to their individual imaginations.

Even when words are clear enough in their principal meanings, annotation could usefully note how a change in an actor's bearing can speak independently or with additional force. Shylock's last words in *The Merchant of Venice* and his lone and silent departure from the stage have already been noticed (p. 27). Malvolio has a somewhat similar exit in *Twelfth Night* when, after 'I'll be revenged on the whole pack of you', he has to relinquish a central position and cross the stage to make his exit. As he goes, or immediately afterwards, Olivia's sympathy – 'He hath been most notoriously abus'd' – will continue to draw the audience's attention to him and to whatever emotion has been expressed: implacable hatred, blind anger, moral indignation, frustration, or confidence in legal processes and his own worth (V.i.365). Stage presence, the timing of speech, and thoughts about what is *not* being said can sometimes influence the effect of unambiguous and simple words. Examples from *Henry the Fourth* are Prince Hal's 'I do, I will', to Falstaff when he is playing the king in a tavern, and King Henry's 'O my son', speaking to Hal shortly before death, and Falstaff's 'Master Shallow, I owe you a thousand pound', after the newly crowned Henry the Fifth has rebuffed his approach (*Part One*, II.iv.464; *Part Two*, IV.v.178 and V.iv.73–4). All these short speeches depend for their effect on the presence of two actors in physical confrontation on stage, their mutual body-language complementing words and speaking in the accompanying verbal silences.

Some simple words and silences are so contained within ongoing dialogue that they might escape a reader's notice unless an editor draws attention to them. In *Hamlet*, for example, nothing in the text refers to the prince's silent presence through the first sixty-four lines of Act I, scene ii; it will, however, be noticed in performance because, like no one else, he is dressed in black and not in the finery appropriate for celebration of a royal marriage. His interjections in the first scene with the Ghost are very explicit but so brief and occasional that his continuous involvement has to be sustained by physical bearing and unspoken reactions (I.v.1–90). For all his many words, Hamlet's presence, developing throughout an actor's performance, will sometimes complicate an audience's response to unremarkable words. It gives substance to such phrases as 'But come' and 'Nay, come, let's go together' to his companions after the Ghost's departure (I.v.168, 191). Towards the end of the play, having said 'how ill all's here about my heart,' he refuses to say more with 'it is no matter ...' and this simple phrase marks Hamlet's withdrawal before using more 'doubtful phrases': 'It is but foolery, but it is such a kind of gain giving as would perhaps trouble a woman' (V.ii.203–9). With these diffident phrases to indicate Hamlet's change of engagement, the actor's physical involvement will help an audience to sense the depths and complexity of his mind. Shortly afterwards, having wrestled verbally with thoughts of augury, providence, and readiness for death, Hamlet breaks off talking with Horatio in a still more secretive way, saying only 'Let be' (l. 217). At this moment. when Hamlet is preparing to fight with Laertes in the presence of the full court, the way the actor speaks and his physical bearing will be more effective than the unremarkable words in marking the switch of feeling and making it credible. Later he varies the same phrase – 'But let it be' (l. 330) – before breaking off to give Horatio the task of publicly reporting the reasons for his actions.

Hamlet's very last words – 'the rest is silence' – also break off from other concerns and disturb syntactical structures. In this final moment, whatever he feels but declines to put into words, whatever weight of conscience he bears within himself, will be more apparent in the actor's entire being than in these ambiguous words. This silent witness can make the strongest impression on an audience when it watches the hero die.[3] What it will be depends on how the actor has reached this moment through the course of the whole play and how each spectator has responded to it. When Hamlet is borne from the stage by four captains, his inert body continues to hold attention and speak silently for all that has happened.

* * *

The fundamental difficulties facing an editor who wishes to annotate a text in order to clarify its life in a theatre have been studied in recent years from the audience's point of view. With colleagues and graduate students at the University of Stockholm, Willmar Sauter has recorded what individual members of the public have said about a great variety of performances including opera, revues and circuses as well as plays by Shakespeare, Calderón, and Molière. From a careful analysis of this detailed evidence one conclusion became increasingly secure: for audiences of all classes and all ages except the very young:

> *How* something is performed is obviously more important than *what* is performed.... . If the spectator is not pleased by the 'how' of the performance, the 'what' becomes secondary and at times even irrelevant. In other words, plot and characters, drama, and text are of little interest unless the overall presentation is satisfying.[4]

If an audience's experience is to be taken into account, it follows that study of a play in performance must consider perception as well as presentation. To quote Sauter again:

in the theatre the 'message' is not something which is neatly packed and distributed to an anonymous consumer; instead, the meaning of a performance is created by the performers and the spectators together, in a joint act of understanding.[5]

This research into what constitutes a theatrical experience recognizes the crucial importance of actors and how they acted, very much as Elizabethan theatregoers did when they wrote or spoke of seeing the players rather than seeing the play. In *The Theatrical Event: Dynamics of Performance and Perception* (2000), Professor Sauter notes that, judged by the huge number of audience responses collected by his teams, 'a spectator only shows interest in the content of a performance when s/he finds the quality of the acting sufficiently high'.[6] This conclusion seems to predicate a specialist audience capable of aesthetic and technical appreciation, but, once a sensory response to acting is considered along with intellectual reactions to a spoken text, appreciation of theatrical performance becomes at least partially instinctive, open to everyone who has feelings, and involving the same faculties as a response to any moment in life itself. Sauter's 'joint act of understanding' between actors and audience does not need to be verbalized or consciously recognized. We respond to actors as we respond to the people we meet, only the operation of our senses is likely to be more intense because the meeting is more clearly defined by a play-text and created by skilled performers.

David Cole's *The Theatrical Event*, written in 1972 and based on first-hand experiences rather than questionnaires and statistics, is more radical in identifying the actor's *presence* before an audience, rather than *performance*, as the unique feature of theatre as an art and the controlling factor in an audience's response. Cole argued that theatre provides 'an opportunity to experience imaginative life as physical presence' and that the actor's body is the agent that makes this possible.[7] Similarly, in 1930, Max Herrmann had argued that 'the shared experience

of real bodies and real space' is the fundamental feature
of theatre as an art form:

> it is the body performing in space which constitutes
> theatre – the actors' bodies moving in and through
> space and the spectators' bodies experiencing the
> spatial dimension of their common environment, the
> particular atmosphere of the space they share and
> their response to the bodily presence of the actors.[8]

These and other studies of what constitutes a theatrical
event argue that words are only one element of a play in
performance and not the one that dominates others in
an audience's response. Any effect that words of dialogue
achieve in a theatre production depends on live actors
present on a stage before an audience, and is mediated
by them in the changing perception of spectators during
the time of performance.

With texts as verbally brilliant as Shakespeare's, editors
will be reluctant to accept that the actors' presence is the
dominant factor in an audience's reception of the plays.
It is in book form that the plays are 'widely acknowledged
as the central achievement of English culture'[9] and so it
would seem reasonable to study them as words on a page.
Until recently it would be assumed that an editor's task
was done when the text was set out with annotations concerning the meaning of words and effect of syntax, together with notes on verbal borrowings, literary
influences, historical allusions, and topical references.
But when the play is performed and holds the attention
of an audience, something more than words and their literary context is involved and those processes have to be
studied with particular care if we wish to understand the
distinctive achievements of Shakespeare's plays. The
almost universal theatrical viability of these texts can
hardly be an accident but must be due to the way in
which they were written. It is therefore reasonable to
assume that, in writing them, Shakespeare imagined his
words being used in performance, with actors playing a
highly significant part in determining their effect on an

audience. If these plays are to be studied as texts intended to be performed, their very variable life on stage has to be taken into account in moments of silence, as it is during speech.

* * *

By seeking to 'present the plays as texts for performances',[10] the General Editors of the latest edition of the Arden Shakespeare have taken on themselves an endless task because, by the time he wrote *Hamlet*, Shakespeare had come to trust actors to express more than he wrote down for them. He knew that they would eventually 'tell all' – as Professor Sauter teaches us to expect – no matter how 'brief' the words they spoke or how hidden their thoughts and instincts might be (III.ii.136–49). Famously, Hamlet has 'that within which passes show', an inner mystery, presence, or state of being that words cannot 'denote ... truly' (I.ii.76–86), and, in this tragedy, other persons are presented in the same way. This is especially true of the two women, perhaps because their reticence was socially expected in those days, or in deference to the capabilities of the young male actors who acted these roles. It is also possible that Shakespeare gave them few words because he wanted to draw a particularly close attention to the unspoken thoughts and inner qualities of the women in the tragedy. Repeatedly, only their presence implies what is happening within them and this is enough to concern Hamlet deeply and influence the main action of the play. An editor presenting the plays as texts for performance will need to annotate much more than words, and explicate silences with care.

At the close of the first of two scenes with her father, Ophelia has been given only 'I shall obey, my lord', and at the close of the second, after being called three times to go with him to the king, she has nothing at all to say (I.iii.136 and II.i.120). In both cases, her father's words ensure that Ophelia is the focus of attention and so, as she walked the five or more metres needed to reach the exit on an Elizabethan stage, her bearing and movements would be watched for whatever unspoken thoughts and feelings they might express. The contrast to her father's bearing and behaviour will ensure that hers, to some degree, will make an effect no matter on what stage the play is performed, particularly since the audience's knowledge of her association with Hamlet will have heightened its curiosity. Ophelia's outspoken and good-humoured advice to her brother and her vivid account of Hamlet's visit to her closet in the same scenes (I.iii.46–51; II.i.77–100) will make her subsequent withdrawal into silence the more noticeable by contrast and more sugges-tive of independent, possibly rebellious, thoughts and feelings

In Act III, scene i, when Hamlet castigates all women with increasing violence, having already denied that he had ever loved Ophelia, the contrast made by her silence about her own feelings when she prays briefly on his behalf will draw at least some attention away from his stream of words: 'O, help him, you sweet heavens! ... O heavenly powers, restore him!' (III.i.134 and 141). Any involuntary or inarticulate cry that Ophelia makes and the inevitable physical signs of her suffering can produce a major effect and draw on an audience's sympathies. Only after Hamlet has left the stage does her speech, in soliloquy, become sustained, controlled, and explicit:

> O, what a noble mind is here o'er thrown! ...
> That unmatch'd form and feature of blown youth
> Blasted with ecstasy. O, woe is me
> To have seen what I have seen, see what I see!
>   (ll. 150–61)

As she now gains the audience's full attention, the king and her father emerge from their place of concealment, talking together about Hamlet. However obvious her wretchedness may be, they both ignore her presence until, for a brief moment, her father breaks off to say 'You need not tell us what Lord Hamlet said; / We heard it all.' To this curt dismissal, she again says nothing at all, her silence now being more remarkable after the preceding soliloquy. Whether she weeps or shows little outward sign of emotion, an audience is likely to feel with her, not with her father or the king, and to be outraged by the way she has been treated. If she makes a hurried exit at this moment, many eyes in the audience will follow her. Alternatively, if she remains on stage and leaves at the end of the scene, taking her own time after Claudius and Polonius have started to go, and in a different direction, she will gain un-divided attention in her silence. In either case, her very presence will make evident the effect of what has amounted to remorseless and unwarranted punishment, at first from Hamlet and then from her father and the king. In any performance of this scene the significance of her silence cannot be missed but a reader may need anno-tation before realizing how attention has been drawn so intently to her that saying nothing can be an expression of a strong will and deep love or, alternatively, of painful defeat, fear, or compliance.

In Ophelia's two mad or distracted appearances in Act IV, scene v, her unspoken thoughts and feelings are made evident by many changes of subject and mood that are otherwise inexplicable. The most affecting silence, because sustained for a long time, is likely to be when she enters for the second time and is faced, unexpectedly, by her brother. He has a lengthy speech while she says nothing to acknowledge his presence, even when addressed directly and lovingly. At first caught up in her own silently tortured and scarcely manageable consciousness she starts to sing, as she had done earlier in the scene, and only then may she address her brother to say farewell,[11] the text being am-biguous about this. She does not leave at this point and what happens next is left very much for other actors on stage to invent or improvise while they all remain silent in response. As she now addresses those around her and then, again, sings, Laertes speaks briefly but now like a chorus, not attempting to communicate: 'Thought and affliction, passion, hell itself, / She turns to favour and to prettiness' (IV.v.184–5). With another abrupt change, Ophelia leaves the stage, praying for 'all Christian souls' (IV.v.196) as if, for the moment, she has found some peace of mind or a new purpose. Although she says nothing of this, some Ophelias will be seen to make this last exit knowing that they are fated to die; others will leave in a way that shows them to be determined to seek release in suicide. Gertrude will later announce her death without resolving this uncertainty (IV.vii.164–5). Among Ophelia's conflicting and discontinuous speeches, and her songs that are often obscure in meaning, Ophelia's innermost feelings, expressed physically and continuously in her presence, are likely to make the strongest impression on an audience in these two prolonged episodes.

An audience is likely to sense at least something of Gertrude's significance in the tragedy on her first silent entry as the bride of Claudius, her second husband. While nothing is said that even alludes to this, some members of an audience in Shakespeare's day would have been aware that marriage to a former husband's brother was against canonical law. Gertrude's silence is also remarkable when, against her advice, Hamlet insists on continuing to mourn publicly for the death of his father. After he has agreed to his mother's 'prayers' that he should stay in the court – 'I shall in all my best obey you, madam' (I.ii.120) – Claudius cuts into their talk as if wanting to prevent further intimacy. As soon as he is alone Hamlet states clearly that his mother's second marriage is the motive for his behaviour and that he must 'hold [his] tongue' about the consequences (l. 159). Although Gertrude has not spoken of her recent marriage, an audience might see physical signs that it is very much in her mind during all her first dealings with both son and second husband. Only in a later scene does she refer briefly to it as one cause of Hamlet's mad behaviour:

> I doubt it is no other but the main,
> His father's death and our o'erhasty marriage.
>
> (II.ii.56–7)

Throughout the entire play Gertrude speaks little compared with other persons and sometimes falls silent when
further speech would be expected. By this means, given
her crucial role in the story, Shakespeare repeatedly drew
an audience's attention to any physical expression she
might give to her silent thoughts. By manipulation of the
audience's attention Shakespeare has ensured that even
the absence of an involuntary clue to her unspoken
thoughts would have been remarkable.

On the one occasion when Gertrude is alone with
Hamlet, in Act III, scene iv, they do eventually talk together in what is, by far, the play's most sustained and
most passionate encounter. At first both are forthright
and antagonistic, quickly angry and impatient of propri-
eties, but Gertrude again falls silent for long stretches,
after Hamlet has killed Polonius, who was hiding behind
an arras. From now on, it is almost always her presence,
not her words, that maintains her part in the ongoing
action. Although she had started by sharply interrogating
Hamlet, she says little in response when he passionately
attacks the sexuality, irrationality, and shamelessness of
her second marriage: 'Stew'd in corruption, honeying
and making love / Over the nasty sty!' (ll. 91–4).
Eventually, begging him to say no more, she admits that
he has forced her to look into her 'very soul' and that his
words have been 'like daggers' in her ears (ll. 88–91,
94–6, 101). In performance the actor must appear physically and strenuously distraught because, when the Ghost
appears to Hamlet to whet his 'almost blunted purpose',
the signs of Gertrude's 'fighting soul' are so obvious that
he orders his son to intervene (ll. 110–15). This 'visita-
tion' finished, Hamlet speaks more 'temperately' than
before and she is now submissive in speech: 'O Hamlet,
thou hast cleft my heart in twain… . What shall I do?'
(ll. 156, 180). Her words are still few and she listens in
silence as her son speaks of 'rank corruption' in her soul,
and of the stale endearments and 'reechy kisses' of 'the
bloat king', imagining him to be 'paddling in [her] neck
with his damned fingers' (ll. 148, 182–6). She has
nothing at all to say when Hamlet proposes to 'lug the

guts into the neighbour room' (l. 212) and so dispose of the corpse of Polonius, the trusted counsellor whom she will soon refer to as the 'good old man' (IV.i.12). Five times Hamlet says 'good night' to his mother and not once does she say a word in reply or acknowledgement, not even when he promises to be at peace with her:

> And when you are desirous to be blest,
> I'll blessing beg of you.
>
> (ll. 171–2)

When Hamlet finally leaves, '*tugging in Polonius*', as the Folio stage direction has it, she still says nothing.

In this scene, generally referred to as 'the closet scene', the extent to which Gertrude appears to suffer in love or sexual desire, for her son or for either of her husbands, or to feel guilt or shame for what she has done, will depend on how the role has been cast and performed. Her very presence, rather than the words she has been given to speak, must sustain her part in most of the encounter. She can seem sensual and weak-willed, or resolutely independent and thoughtful. She may respond more with sighs and tears than with expressions of terror or love. She can become more physically intimate with her son or draw further apart. Hamlet contributes many violent and hurtful words but both participants are responsible for the progress of the scene, its almost savage emotional charge, and its culminating resolution. The scene holds attention most strongly when the two actors, in different ways, are almost equally matched in stage presence and instinctive reactions to each other. Annotation of this centrally placed meeting between son and mother cannot give an adequate impression of the play in performance without explaining how it depends on the deep-seated qualities of two actors and the silences of Gertrude.

The next scene starts with Claudius asking her to 'translate' her 'sighs [and] profound heaves' (IV.i.1–2), which probably implies she has remained on stage, as the Arden and other editors suggest. She may appear so shamed and broken in spirit that an audience will believe her to be incapable of moving or doing anything at all and yet, after a silence indicated by an incomplete verse-line, her first words are to ask for privacy: 'Bestow this place on us a little while' (IV.i.4). That done, she follows her son's instruction and tells Claudius that Hamlet is uncontrollably mad, not 'mad in craft' as she now knows him to be (IV.i.5–12 and III.iv.187–90). Unexpectedly, in her son's absence, she has regained control of herself and takes a vocal part in the dangerous and rapidly changing situation.

In later scenes, Gertrude's power over both Claudius and Hamlet becomes more evident in performance. When her husband calls her three times to 'come away' and acknowledges the 'discord and dismay' in his soul (IV.i. 28, 38, 44–5), she again makes no verbal response but any resistance to his pressure, by delaying the move or leaving after him, will mark an increasing separation between wife and husband that is entirely of her choosing. After Ophelia's first mad scene, Claudius again asks for her sympathy:

> O Gertrude, Gertrude!
> When sorrows come, they come not single spies,
> But in battalions!
>
> (IV.v.74–6)

Despite the silence indicated by the opening half-line and the note of appeal implicit in the repetition of her name, Gertrude again makes no verbal reply but is almost sure to respond in some other way. From this point onwards she will seem more self-controlled than either Claudius or Hamlet. At Ophelia's burial, when Hamlet fights with Laertes so that they have to be plucked apart, it is Gertrude, and neither Claudius nor Horatio, who tries to reason with him and, eventually, brings him to admit, 'I loved Ophelia' (V.i.263). When he again challenges Laertes, she is the one who calms him with a tender and maternal simile:

> This is mere madness;
> And thus awhile the fit will work on him;

> Anon, as patient as the female dove
> When that her golden couplets are disclos'd,[12]
> His silence will sit drooping.

(ll. 278–82)

At once he is reasonable, able now to view events objectively and in their long gestation:

> Hear you, sir:
> What is the reason that you use me thus?
> I lov'd you ever... .

(ll. 282–84)

Mother and son having, at last, been close and verbally intimate, even in a crowded and dangerous situation, the play's action moves forward towards its conclusion. The effect of this meeting derives from a sequence of encounters earlier in the play and the accumulating evidence of a compelling physical relationship that both experience in each other's presence and seldom need to identify in words. While audiences will respond instinctively to the progressive revelations of their feelings for each other, readers would be helped by annotations that demonstrated how silences and other features in the plotting of the play have a major influence on an audience's experience and understanding.

* * *

Study of silences that occur where speech might be expected and of speeches that use the simplest of verbal means can clarify the involvement of the persons in these moments and will often give insights into how the play is structured and the issues that become dominant in performance. Seeing a production or reading records of notable performances will show how the simple words can be spoken and the silences sustained, and thereby demonstrate the importance of these moments and some of their meanings and implications. Practical exploration of a number of different ways in which a simple speech could be spoken –

however skilled, unskilled or unlikely the renderings – will often set imagination to work and encourage a more critical view of the text. Any silence that is marked in some way, by occurring on an exit perhaps or when a preceding speech has called for some verbal response, should be related to how the performance has developed so far in the play and especially to moments when the person now being silent has used words freely. What he or she says and does afterwards will also be relevant, and how others react at the moment. Silences are significant not only in the presentation of the leading persons in the drama but also in building or deflecting the audience's expectation of what is about to happen or what may happen in a more distant future or beyond the bounds of the action. Rather than being times when the author has given little or no instruction to the actor, they should be seen as occasions when the cast and their audiences are encouraged to take the widest view of what is happening and to respond accordingly. The same is true of some verbally simple speeches. Their theatrical potential is so great that they call for detailed analysis and imaginative exploration in any study of the plays.

Notes

1. With kind permission, this chapter is a development and revision of an essay with the same title in Ann Thompson and Gordon McMullan (eds), *In Arden: Editing Shakespeare* (London: Thomson Learning, 2003), pp. 157–74. Where annotations are quoted in this chapter, references are to each specified edition.
2. For example, see the ending of *As You Like It*, described in Chapter 1, pp. 19–20, above.

3. Hamlet's last words are followed in the Folio text with 'O, o, o, o. *Dyes*'. The Arden editor considers this an interpolation, indicating that, in early performances, the actor would die making an audible response. Later scholars have been more inclined to accept the four vowels as an authorial addition to an earlier version. George Hibbard, in the Oxford edition of 1987, translated them into a stage direction: '*He gives a long sigh and dies.*'

4. Willmar Sauter, *The Theatrical Event: Dynamics of Performance and Perception* (Iowa City: University of Iowa Press, 2000), p. 49.

5. Ibid., p. 2.

6. Ibid., p. 49.

7. David Cole, *The Theatrical Event: A Mythos, a Vocabulary, a Perspective* (Middletown, CT: Wesleyan University Press, 1975), Introduction, p. x.

8. The translated quotation and the subsequent summing-up of Hermann's argument are taken from Erika Fischer-Lichte, 'From Text to Performance: The Rise of Theatre Studies as an Academic Discipline in Germany', *Theatre Research International*, vol. 24, no. 2 (1999), pp. 171–2.

9. Stephen Greenblatt, *Shakespearean Negotiations: The Circulation of Social Energy in Renaissance England* (Oxford: Oxford University Press, 1988), pp. 160–1.

10. *King Lear*, ed. R. A. Foakes, the Arden Shakespeare (Walton-on-Thames: Thomas Nelson, 1997), 'General Editors' Preface', p. xv. For a discussion of this intention, see George Walton Williams, 'To edit? To direct?' in Thompson and McMullan, *In Arden: Editing Shakespeare*, especially pp. 111–12.

11. So the Arden's annotation argues; in the Folio the words of farewell are printed as part of the song, and in the Second Quarto they are not distinguishable from it.

12. That is, when her pair of golden-coloured chicks are hatched.

4

Accounting for Space: Choreography

Play-texts only record the words to be spoken and a few stage directions, some of doubtful authenticity, and so it may seem that Shakespeare has left little guidance about staging for present-day actors and directors. But, on the contrary, implicit in the dialogue is a network of instructions that, in today's language, can be called the choreography of each play. Shakespeare was very knowledgeable about physical performance. He wrote for a company of actors with whom he had daily dealings over long periods of time. In his formative years he had acted among them on stage in a large repertoire of plays that included his own. As a consequence, when he wrote dialogue he would have seen actors in his mind's eye, aware of how they might move and interact with each other. If we read the texts with open eyes, we can trace the imprint of this very close and specialized knowledge, an awareness as lively and careful as his understanding of words and speech.

A stage would also have been present in his mind as he wrote, most often one at the Theatre or the Globe and, later, the rather different one at the Blackfriars. The most important feature these stages had in common was an open space in close contact with an audience standing or sitting on several sides and in the same light as the actors. Little else could be relied on because the Chamberlain's and King's Men would also go on tour to less predictable or suitable venues, such as a hall in one of several royal palaces or that of a great house, university, grammar school, or lawyers' inn, or in a guild house, market hall or town hall; occasionally they would perform in a convenient place out of doors. In Shakespeare's mind the stage was pre-eminently a clear space in which actors could move freely and be at all times the object of attention for an audience less than fifty feet away. The guidance he gave about positioning, movement, and timing had to be adaptable to spaces of different sizes and shapes and was therefore mostly concerned with the relationship of actors to each other and their movements, both in groups and individually. Because of frequent changes of plays in a large repertoire, he would have known that a degree of uncertainty about where to go would always be present and need scope for improvisation. This free and open choreography, but basically ordered none the less, was well suited to the quick-moving freedom of his mind as expressed in the dialogue of the plays.[1]

* * *

In some respects, however, the configuration common to the London theatres has left clear traces in the choreography of the plays. Among a more general flux of motion, made almost continuous by the actors' need to be heard and seen from several sides, two fixed points of entry through the permanent façade of the tiring house at either side of the rear of the stage provided two points, in strong positions for drawing attention, that were used to emphasize and define particular moments in a play's action. A third central entrance was used more occasionally to reveal or 'discover' large stage properties or groups of persons by opening curtains. It was also available for entries that were impressively large in scale. When the company was on tour and acted on a stage backed by the screen of a dining or assembly hall, two entries at either side would often be in place ready for use. A larger, central entrance would probably require

some temporary structure and hangings. If the company
had to act on a freestanding platform, a row of curtains
would have been set up at the rear to give the necessary
entrances. With little else invariably present, the two
points of access at opposite sides to the rear of the acting
area were a major resource on all stages. By drawing the
audience's eyes away from centre stage, an entry would
visually emphasize a person's change of mind, health,
or fortune, the passage of time, or a change of locale.

As noted in Chapter 2, unexpected entries, especially of
persons new to the play, were used to alert an audience to
reports of events not represented on stage and to new per-
ceptions of the current situation.[2] They could also have a
large visual effect by altering the posture, position, and behaviour of everyone on stage. For example, Marcade's unexpected and unannounced entry during the 'merriment'
of Act V, scene ii, of *Love's Labour's Lost* (l. 703) immediately 'interrupts' the scene, altering its tone, content, and
physical alignments, while the dialogue changes from
prose to short-phrased, simply-worded verse:

MARCADE   God save you, madam!
PRINCESS   Welcome, Marcade;
     But that thou interruptest our merriment.
MARCADE   I am sorry, madam; for the news I bring
     Is heavy in my tongue. The King your father –
PRINCESS   Dead, for my life!
MARCADE   Even so; my tale is told.
BEROWNE   Worthies, away; the scene begins to cloud.
                                (V.ii.703–8)

With Armado the one courageous exception, the actors
of the 'show' that is in progress go off stage without a
word and the Princess herself is speechless until the
King asks 'How fares your Majesty?' She has no words to
answer him but turns away to order preparations for
leaving Navarre that night. As every word is coloured by
her 'new-sad soul' (l. 719), everyone on stage will
behave under the same cloud, moving and regrouping
as the new business requires. Improvisation, uncertainty,

clumsiness, and prolonged silences will be among the extended fall-out of this unexpected entry.

By his late entry, Jaques de Boys springs a surprise to quite different effect at the end of *As You Like It.* No one answers his abrupt request for a hearing but he continues by announcing that he is the second son of old Sir Rowland, a person not seen before in the play and whose existence has been mentioned only once in the very first moments of its first scene. In freely flowing words he reports that the usurping tyrant, Duke Frederick, has raised a mighty army to capture and put to death the rightful duke, his brother. This alarming news will be spoken with a contrasting composure because, before anyone can reply, he reports the villain's sudden conversion and subsequent abdication. Those who are listening will not know how to take these amazing changes of fortune and so, as if afraid of not being believed, Jaques pledges his life on the truth of his news. That proves enough for the rightful duke to welcome him and the good fortune he brings to everyone assembled. They all turn attention to celebrations as the Duke orders dancing and rustic revelry: 'With measure heap'd in joy, to th' measures fall' (V.iv.160–73). Spirits have risen as if by magic but now, as partners come together and music plays, the other, 'melancholy' Jaques who has often been an independent figure in the forest, resists the joyful infection. After he has delivered a valedictory speech and refused the Duke's plea to stay, the forward action of the comedy is held back for his lonely departure through the very entrance that has just revealed the new arrival bearing the same name as himself. The Duke then sets all in motion again:

> Proceed, proceed. We will begin these rites,
> As we do trust they'll end, in true delights.

Dancing follows until the festive company leaves the stage, Rosalind being the single exception. She stays behind, or immediately returns to the stage to speak an Epilogue, both as an actor and as Rosalind.

At the end of both these comedies, the ordering of persons on stage is disturbed when an unexpected entry is made and new dispositions have to follow. Without lengthy rehearsal all the other actors will have to improvise as the persons they play find their own accommodation to what has been reported. Visually the focus will be uncertain until new business is under way and the comedy moves to its conclusion. In *Love's Labour's Lost*, this resolution is tentative and calls for 'honest plain words' (V.ii.741), and, even then, it is not complete: 'Our wooing doth not end like an old play: / Jack hath not Jill' (ll. 862–3). Songs are introduced to complete the comedy with the entire actors' company on stage. This communal event is introduced by Armado, the knight whose performance as Hector in *'The Pageant of the Worthies'* had ended shamefully.[3] His re-entry as leader of the unskilled actors will be the comedy's last surprising entry and his appearance will now be very different. He had left the stage promising to 'right [him]self like a soldier' (V.ii.711–13) but now Jaquenetta, the young and pregnant country wench, will be at his side while songs of the Owl and Cuckoo tell of spring time and winter and of cuckoldry and love. At the end of *As You Like It*, Jaques prefaces his exit from the celebrations by pronouncing judgement on each pair of lovers and the Duke. As for himself, he says that he has much to hear and learn from the convertite, who has 'thrown into neglect the pompous court' (V.iv.175–6), that well-established society to which the other exiles are about to return. In both comedies, words speak of a need for trust and self-content while, visually, improvised re-arrangements on stage will show the tentative nature of these resolutions.

* * *

Besides changing the expectations and grouping of persons already on stage, the strong focus that entries attract can also alter the parameters of a play by enlarging the imagined space in which it is taking place.

Macbeth, in this and other ways a spectacular tragedy, has a sequence of these devices. A '*bleeding* Sergeant', at the start of Act I, scene ii, meets the king and brings the visual evidence of his own wounds to augment his account of an off-stage battle. He is on the point of exhaustion and, as his 'gashes cry for help', he has to be helped from the stage (I.ii.43–5). By this means, before Macbeth enters the play, visual evidence evokes the bloodshed of a distant battle, and a painful struggle to speak presents a physical contrast to the security and ordered business of Scotland's king and his attendants. At the start of Act I, scene vii, the Folio text has the stage direction, '*Enter a Sewer, and divers Servants with Dishes and Service* [*passing*] *over the stage,*' which requires movement on stage, accompanied by torches and the music of hautboys. Choreographically this provides a visual demonstration of the lavish feast that welcomes the king to Macbeth's castle, the home in which his murder is being planned. The more elaborate and unhurried the entry and exit of these un-named servants are made, the wider the imaginary perspective in which the audience will view Macbeth in the very next moment, when he enters alone, speaking of murder and appalled at the crime he is about to commit.

At the beginning of the following scene the Folio reads '*Enter Banquo, and Fleance, with a Torch before him.*' The first words are Banquo's, 'How does the night, boy?' which probably implies that Fleance, on this first entry to the play, walks ahead of his father and carries the torch: an unexpected and entirely new physical presence. When Banquo unbuckles his sword to give to Fleance and speaks of his fears in going to bed, it becomes clear that this 'boy' is his son. Words are few and simple but the young voice and presence contrast strongly with those of Banquo and of Macbeth, who enters immediately afterwards: compared with them, he knows almost nothing and can move more freely. The two battle-hardened soldiers were first seen close together as fellow 'captains', and later, the king had held Banquo to his heart as one 'no less deserv'd' than Macbeth (I.ii.34 and I.iv.29–31), but now, after their encounter with the witches and no longer dressed for battle, they are seen to be watchful of each other, in opposition rather than comradeship. They are also separated by Macbeth's intention to murder the king as a means of gaining the crown and by his lack of such a personal and trusted attendant as Fleance. In the way Macbeth and Banquo physically encounter each other, an audience may see more than either of them acknowledges in words and more than Banquo realizes at this time.

After the murder of Duncan a succession of independent entries and exits express widespread and varied alarm. The drunken Porter, behaving as if he were in hell, starts the action as Lennox and Macduff knock repeatedly at the castle gate. Their clothes, as well as everything they say and do, will show that these men have been riding through the night in a storm of unusual force. Then Macbeth enters alone after a sleepless night during which he has murdered the king. An assumed normality will at least partly hide what is uppermost in his mind – the horror, guilt, and fear which, moments earlier, the audience had seen render him powerless. Watching Macduff leave to go to Duncan's lodging, Macbeth knows what will be found and dares not speak of it and yet, to an account of the 'unruly' night, he has to respond or awaken suspicion. However earnestly or apprehensively the 'young' Lennox recounts his experience (II.iii.60), the audience's visual focus, during this time of waiting, is bound to return to Macbeth, who says nothing at first: mentally he will seem frozen up, gripped by unspoken, unspeakable terror. Lennox brings a contrasting physical energy and freedom so that Macbeth's four brief words in reply – ''Twas a rough night' (l. 59) – can either wryly and humorously express the obvious, or touch the depth of his true feelings; some actors find that both these responses arise simultaneously. Physical performance and movements on and off stage have ensured that the audience will be watching closely enough to notice the smallest sign of fear or guilt. When Macduff re-enters he is transformed by what he has seen, his cry sounding like a great drum or deep trumpet, at once threatening and stunned: 'O horror, horror, horror!' Arrival on stage through the entrance now associated with the king's bedchamber, and the subsequent change of everyone's focus, call for the actor's total commitment to what Macduff has seen off stage, so that a genuine horror is heard in his threefold cry and seen in his laboured breathing and shaken bearing. Renewing his energy and at last finding more words, even while knowing them to be inadequate, he sends Macbeth and Lennox to see for themselves while he raises the alarm and calls for a bell to be rung. When Shakespeare was writing the fragmented dialogue for this episode, he must have envisioned all this happening in his mind's eye.

Alone on the stage Macduff must wait for others. As he calls other sleepers to join him, his words are repetitive, direct and strong, but varied by ideas and images that arise along with more immediate and practical reactions: natural death, the great doom, graves, and walking spirits. For the moment, one horror-struck, active and morally aware man represents the entire play, its story made palpable in and through him. An audience could not have expected this because only moments before, Macduff had spoken the first words he has in the play while his arrival was being up-staged and eclipsed, first by the Porter and then by Macbeth. Later in the action, this person, now almost unknown, will escape from Scotland, risking and losing all he holds dear, and then return to seek out Macbeth and kill him. Macduff cannot know this future but an audience might sense it because the actor cannot help being aware of it every time the play is re-hearsed and performed. Within this lone figure, that the play's choreography picks out as if with a spotlight, the ending of the play lies coiled at a deep and hidden level of consciousness, ready for release.

The focus now shifts repeatedly as many entries follow. First Lady Macbeth and then Banquo come on stage; next, Macbeth and Lennox. Ross also appears, probably at another entrance, and others too in sufficient numbers to 'carry out' Lady Macbeth a few moments later. Among all these dispersed and urgent movements, every person having risen from their beds only partly dressed or with blankets caught up around them in alarm and fear, an audience will scarcely know where to look. That does not last for long because all eyes on stage will begin to fasten on Macbeth, who comes from the scene of murder and speaks words that both hide his guilt and give a foretaste of a sense of loss and futility that will haunt him at the end of the tragedy:[4]

> Had I but died an hour before this chance,
> I had liv'd a blessed time; for, from this instant,
> There's nothing serious in mortality –
> All is but toys; renown and grace is dead;
> The wine of life is drawn, and the mere lees
> Is left this vault to brag of.
>
> (II.iii.89–94)

Macbeth has found a new way of speaking and his physical bearing will bear signs of what he has seen and done while he was off stage. The act of re-entry will emphasize the change but, with Malcolm and Donalbain coming on stage as he finishes speaking, any exposure of the workings of his mind will be brief. Almost immediately he is faced with the task of explaining why he has killed the two grooms who were guarding Duncan. As he describes the king's mangled corpse and speaks of his love for him, Lady Macbeth faints and that surprise and silent action causes the focus of attention to change yet again. In performance the actor will have to choose whether this faint is real or a pretence. She could be shielding her husband by deflecting attention when she hears him speak of feelings that had earlier threatened his resolve, or her fainting could be an involuntary sign of her own weakness and a foretaste of the 'unnatural troubles' that will draw her to a tormented death (V.i.69–72). Either way, Macbeth stops speaking, perhaps stunned or perhaps relieved of the need to continue: it is Macduff who again takes charge at centre stage, calling for others to help the lady.

As Lady Macbeth is carried out, turmoil and uncertainty are brought under control, not by Macbeth or

Macduff but by Banquo, who has said nothing so far in this scene, except immediately upon entrance. Now his clear thinking and straight speaking will hold attention, with everyone on stage facing towards him:

> … when we have our naked frailties hid,
> That suffer in exposure, let us meet,
> And question this most bloody piece of work,
> To know it further. Fears and scruples shake us… .

Only a few more words are spoken before everyone leaves, excepting the two sons of Duncan. They remain on an otherwise empty stage for rapid and frightened discussion, before hurrying off to different destinations to escape danger.

Besides carrying dramatic action forward, the varied entries and exits, with a continual regrouping of all the persons on stage, have given visual expression to fears and scruples that only Banquo subsequently acknowledges. The effect is to unsettle an audience, not least because Macbeth, having committed the crime, loses the central position on stage while Banquo makes the one call for counter-action and follows that with a declaration of his trust in a more than mortal power. At first, Macbeth merely agrees with him, along with everyone else:

> BANQUO   … Fears and scruples shake us.
>   In the great hand of God I stand, and thence
>   Against the undivulg'd pretence I fight
>   Of treasonous malice.
> MACDUFF   And so do I.
> ALL   So all.

Then, at last, Macbeth takes over briefly, concentrating on the need for action:

> MACBETH   Let's briefly put on manly readiness
>   And meet i' th' hall together.
> ALL   Well contented.
>   [*Exeunt*]

The diminishing of Macbeth's contribution to the
action is arguably the scene's most revealing feature. It
happens gradually, as if by chance and without a verbal
decision, but clarified in wordless performance and by
a choreography that involves everyone. The call for immediate action, with which Macbeth draws the scene to
a close and obliterates other thoughts, will be repeated
in a very different form at a yet more crucial moment
when, deserted by everyone else, he faces certain
death: 'Lay on, Macduff;/And damn'd be him that first
cries "Hold, enough!"' (V.viii.33–4). When the audience sees him draw strength from action here it may
receive a premonition of the tragic ending; for the
actor, this is a preparatory step in a long and deep-set
process.

Act II, scene iv, provides an immediate contrast,
having little action, careful words, and only three
persons on stage. As soon as Ross enters, unannounced,
not saying a word but listening to an unnamed person –
in the stage direction and speech-prefixes he is simply
an 'Old Man' – an audience may sense a mysterious ordering of events. Speaking together of strange portents,
man's misdeeds, and the threatening heavens over a
'bloody stage', neither one identifies the location or explains why they have come together. When Macduff
joins them, also without explanation, he speaks exclusively to Ross, as if the Old Man were not present or not
trusted to hear what is said. Their talk is about Duncan's
murder, Macbeth's slaying of the king's two grooms, and
the escape of his two sons, all matters only mentioned
vaguely, previously in this scene, as an 'unnatural …
deed' (ll. 10–11). Unheralded entries for unspecified
reasons, separate discussions, and dialogue at first im-
personally allusive and then tersely direct, may all mark
this meeting as taking place where talk would be dangerous if too open or specific. When Ross and Macduff
leave to two different destinations, the Old Man's words
suggest that the location may have been a chapel and
the underlying intentions of those present moral and
political:

> God's benison go with you, and with those
> That would make good of bad, and friends of foes.
>
> (ll. 40–1)

Ross has addressed the Old Man as 'good father' and
'father', words commonly used of priests and friars;[5] and
his costume and manner might well indicate that this is
the sense intended here. If Ross kneels to be blessed
before he goes to witness Macbeth's coronation at Scone,
their parting will give the audience a momentary view of
a more peaceful and trusting way of life.

In this short scene and elsewhere, choreography is a
powerful factor in establishing a wide context for this
tragedy. In the Witches' four scenes, including the very
first of the play, their movements 'round about' and their
repetitive ritualistic actions will physically demonstrate
the corporate power of an 'alternative' existence. Here
the choreography may hold an audience's attention more
strongly and consistently than the weird details of what is
spoken. The next Witches' scene, in which Hecate enters
the play and addresses them for thirty lines without interruption (Act III, scene v), may seem on first reading to be
an exception to this, but visually this too is impressive.
The goddess enters alone, without any previous notice,
and she may have 'descended' from above.[6] Before saying
anything, her mere presence is enough to make the First
Witch declare that she looks 'angerly' (l. 1). When she
berates the Witches for being 'saucy and overbold', they
submit to her harsh judgement. If they now behave as
they did in earlier scenes, all three will react physically
and appropriately to each clearly marked phase of
Hecate's speech: its reproofs and vaunting, and the
promise of 'great business' for which they must prepare.
Hecate's report of flying to the moon widens the context
of the action and, finally, her intention of drawing
Macbeth 'to his confusion' will almost certainly be
greeted with signs of approval and anticipation. To all
this there is no verbal response but from their silent ser-
vility we may conclude that the Witches react in the
dynamic and outwardly demonstrative style of earlier

scenes. They will move both individually and in unison, crouching together in fear or scattering to escape punishment. They may cower, stone-still, and then move quickly to show that they will 'make amends' and start their preparations. They could hear Hecate's promises in excited obeisance and then, finally and climactically, dance together in anticipation of victory. In other plays Shakespeare calls for strong physical responses to the manifestation of supernatural power: in *A Midsummer Night's Dream*, Puck shows eye-catching and swift obedience to Oberon, and in *The Tempest*, Caliban cringes before Prospero, Gonzalo speaks of the 'ecstasy' gripping his spellbound enemies, and Ariel reports on their distraction as his charm 'strongly works 'em'; in the last scene of the play, a spellbound Alonzo returns to the stage '*with a frantic gesture*'.[7] If the Witches react to Hecate in the instinctive, corporate, and physically demonstrative manner of their earlier appearances, when all three wound up their charm by chanting and dancing and laid fingers to lips to hail Macbeth and Banquo in chorus, their reactions here will take attention almost as strongly as the words that Hecate speaks – completely so, should she pause to take notice of them.[8]

Although the Witches do not enter in the last Act, their influence on Macbeth has never been stronger. The cutting of green branches to hide the number of opposing forces is the most eye-catching fulfilment of their prophecies but an audience will also see that Macbeth, in thought and action, follows the course that Hecate had promised:

> He shall spurn fate, scorn death, and bear
> His hopes 'bove wisdom, grace, and fear.
>
> (III.v.30–1)

He considers alternatives but then does as she has foretold, as if he cannot do otherwise. His entries and exits make this strikingly clear. He comes on stage four times within 207 lines, an exceptional frequency for anyone in any of the plays, and each time he enters onto an empty stage, seeking no one and giving no reason why he should come at this time or to this place. Nor is it clear why he leaves or where he is going. Macbeth moves without another thought, as if under compulsion like an automaton. At first he is followed by an unspecified number of 'Attendants' but these drop away, as the Thanes are reported to have done already, and on his last two entrances he is alone. The Doctor who had attended his wife is with him at first but leaves at the end of the first scene, fearing for his own safety. Seyton has to be called three times before joining Macbeth; he probably brings Macbeth's armour with him but, when asked for it, says that it is 'not needed yet' (V.iii.33). Sent to find the cause of an off-stage cry he returns with news of the queen's death and then is gone without a word to mark his departure. As noted already, his very name can sound ominous (see pp. 61–2, above). Choreographically Macbeth's progressive isolation makes visible a closing of options, as if some fate and the consequence of his own actions are bearing down upon him. Inevitably, it seems, he is beyond the reach of anyone's help.

What happens in Macbeth's last moments is uncertain. At the point where he and Macduff join in the final combat something is amiss with the Folio stage direction: '*Exeunt fighting. Alarums. // Enter fighting, and Macbeth slain.*' If the killing is on stage as this requires, Macduff will have to leave dragging the dead body after him and re-enter later to display Macbeth's decapitated head as the Folio also requires. Perhaps the last few words of a stage direction are missing and the two should leave the stage a second time with Macbeth wounded but not yet dead. Some present-day productions solve the textual problem by ignoring the direction to '*Enter fighting*' but, if retained in some form, the return will accentuate the seemingly enforced nature of Macbeth's movements on and off stage throughout the last Act, the pace and effort redoubled in a desperate endeavour to fight until the inevitable end. Macduff's arrival bearing the severed head will, in any case, offer a bloody and disfigured object in place of the tragedy's previously resourceful

hero. As at the end of *Richard the Second,* where the hero's
last entry is in his coffin, Shakespeare has left the audience with a static and physical image that challenges its
ability to understand. For both these plays, in the last
resort, the players do not 'tell all';[9] in *Macbeth,* as noted in
the previous chapter (pp. 66–72), silence becomes an essential element of the tragedy, together with the sight of
the bloody head of a murderous tyrant and a victorious
army giving allegiance to a new king. Audiences who
have been drawn by many sensitive words to think and
feel with the workings of the hero's mind are given no
words now that will help them to reconcile that sense of
kinship with their horror at Macbeth's inhumanity and
the consequences of his crimes. Shakespeare has written
the tragedy so that any comprehensive judgement is the
audience's responsibility and is likely to be unavoidable.

* * *

Rudolph Arnheim's *The Power of the Center* (1988)[10] starts
by demonstrating that the centre of any visual composition strongly attracts attention, a phenomenon that is
'deeply rooted in human nature and ultimately in the
very make up of the nervous system we all have in
common' (pp. 2–3). Consequently, changes at the centre
of what happens on stage are especially significant and
can subconsciously influence an audience's response to
theatrical performance. In these matters Shakespeare's
invention was varied and resourceful, controlling the
focus of attention at every turn of a story and, on occasion, calling into question where the centre of power is to
be found.

Returning to *Hamlet* for example, we find that its three
scenes that are located at court and involve almost all the
cast are configured in three different ways, the last
echoing and significantly varying previously established
stage-images.[11] In the first, Claudius, with a mostly silent
Gertrude at his side, holds pride of place as the person
possessing greatest power, while Hamlet settles himself

off-centre and, as the second Quarto has it, '*cum aliis*'. He is briefly drawn into the centre but only commands the stage when everyone else has left and he can speak freely for himself. The second court scene has two centres, one occupied by the players performing the play-within-the-play and the other, as before, by Claudius and Gertrude. Hamlet has refused to join his mother but has again placed himself off-centre where he can watch both '*The Mousetrap*' in performance and the king; he has also placed the silent Horatio to watch Claudius from another position. Only when the double centres have been disturbed and the court has left, does Hamlet again take and hold the centre: now, at last, the play's forward action depends almost entirely upon him. The third court scene also has two centres. Claudius and Gertrude are once again a powerful focus for attention· but, instead of a fictional play, the other centre is the increasingly dangerous duel between Hamlet and Laertes, who, with the king's connivance, seeks revenge for his father's death by whatever means he has been able to contrive. The visual balance is broken, as that of the previous court scene had been, but this time repeatedly: by Gertrude's movement towards her son to 'wipe [his] face' (V.ii.286), by her drinking of poison and her painful death, and then, still more strongly, by the 'incensed' fighting (l. 293) that will eventually draw all attention. When the queen and Laertes are both dead, Hamlet moves to the king and, with no one intervening, becomes the centre of the composition as he revenges his father's death. Hamlet holds that position until his own death, by which time Fortinbras and his army have been heard approaching: soon they will provide an alternative focus of attention to Hamlet's dead body.

The repeated presence of Hamlet at the border of the stage-space and yet related to its centre has an emphasis or weight that uses another principle of visual composition, its effect increased because his clothes are entirely black in contrast to those of every other person. As Arnheim puts it, 'the potential energy inherent in an object grows as that object moves away from the center of attraction'.[12] In the Play Scene, Hamlet's provocative and bawdy talk with Ophelia, entirely contrary to the composure of other spectators, is likely to draw an off-centre attention, as if Shakespeare had wanted to demonstrate this onlooker's heightened sexual responses as the play is about to be enacted and to contrast this with the more passive interest shown by others. As Arnheim notes, an object's resistance to the power of the centre is perceived as additional weight or potential energy:

> One can understand this phenomenon by thinking of the object as attached to the center of attraction by a rubber band. The farther removed it is from the center, the more resistance it has to overcome.[13]

Once the play has started, Hamlet's interruption of the actors' performance emphasizes his impatience by threatening both the centres of the composition as well as the progress of '*The Mousetrap*': 'Begin murderer; pox, leave thy damnable faces and begin. Come; the croaking raven doth bellow for revenge' (III.ii.247–9). Soon, as the player pours poison in the victim's ear, Hamlet waits no more and, in effect, takes over as the second centre in place of the enacted play. In turn, this disturbance triggers Claudius's total disruption of the other and more static centre:

> HAMLET 'A poisons him i' th' garden for his estate.
> His name's Gonzago. The story is extant, and
> written in very choice Italian. You shall see anon
> how the murderer gets the love of Gonzago's wife.
> OPHELIA The King rises.
> HAMLET What, frighted with false fire!
> QUEEN How fares my lord?
> POLONIUS Give o'er the play.
> KING Give me some light. Away!
> POLONIUS Lights, lights, lights!

(ll. 255–64)

Hamlet has revealed his own very personal and irresistible concern with the play that Claudius is watching, his account of it culminating in the second marriage of the fictional queen, which mirrors his mother's remarriage. By having Claudius leave the stage at this point Shakespeare has ensured that it is not '*The Mousetrap*' that 'catch[es] the conscience of the King' (II.ii.601) as Hamlet had intended, but rather, Hamlet himself who takes over from the fictional play as the real-life son of a murdered king. While the players disperse and take their stage properties with them, Hamlet remains on stage with Horatio, the other witness he had placed off-centre. By disturbing the two centres of the composition, Shakespeare's choreography shows that it is Hamlet's sexual impulses and filial feelings that drive the action forward. The tragedy's intellectual themes – its moral, philosophical and political issues – are presented in many more words than these other compulsions but an audience is given powerful visual and kinetic evidence of them at this time, when they are unnamed and unnameable.

* * *

Although not always evident to a reader because occurring over a period of time and without verbal identification, a recurrence of certain physical activities on stage can give a sense of authority to the progress of events or a seeming inevitability to their outcome. Even a single visual repetition can demonstrate the nature of an action in ways that the persons involved cannot mention or do not recognize. When repetition brings a significant difference from the previous occurrence, a play's narrative can be wordlessly clarified or taken a purposeful leap forward. The repeated entrances and exits for Macbeth, noticed a few pages back, offer examples of all these effects.

In the comedies, with their multiple story-lines and assorted lovers, the recurrence of certain visual effects is often clearly marked in the dialogue so that a reader can be in no doubt that Shakespeare knew and valued the power of repetition. In Act IV of *Love's Labour's Lost*, the king and two fellow votaries come forward, one after another, to read the verses they have composed to their mistresses and to be overheard and mocked by Berowne, who eventually is revealed as another lover and verse-maker. In *Much Ado*, first Benedick and then Beatrice overhears the talk of others that is intended to trick them into believing that each one is admired and beloved by the other. Near the end of *As You Like It*, Phebe calls on Sylvius to tell Rosalind 'what 'tis to love' and a declaration follows that is repetitive itself and provokes repetitive agreement from all listeners. Rosalind intervenes with, 'Pray you, no more of this; 'tis like the howling of Irish wolves against the moon' (V.ii.102–4), and immediately starts another series of repetitions with her own promises, which are carefully and mysteriously phrased: these have no verbal responses but all present will react physically in varied and revealing ways. Two scenes later, two other series of pronouncements cover much the same ground, the first shared between a number of speakers, the second spoken by Jaques as a valedictory judgement on the assembled lovers, whose non-verbal responses will contribute at least as much and as variously as the words that they hear and that the audience will anticipate.

When a number of physical repetitions lead an audience to expect yet further instances, the breaking of that series can attract close attention and mark the innovation unmistakably. In *Othello*, for instance, as early as Act III when Othello vows revenge for what he takes to be Desdemona's unfaithfulness and calls Iago to look as he blows away 'all my fond love', he responds physically as well, his bosom swelling with 'tyrannous hate' (III.iii.446–66). Two scenes later, tortured and murderous passion cause his body to shake until, gasping for breath and broken in speech, he '*falls in a trance*' (IV.i.31–43). When he insults his wife in public and strikes her, his retched out 'Goats and monkeys!' (IV.i.260) is a presage of still more uncontrollable and bestial reactions. Just before the final scene, further repetition of physical violence is promised when Othello speaks of a quick and brutal killing:

> Strumpet, I come.
> Forth of my heart those charms, thine eyes, are blotted;
> Thy bed, lust-stain'd, shall with lust's blood be spotted.
>   (V.i.34–6)

But as a trailer for the murder, these words and earlier actions are deceptive because, as he comes to Desdemona's bedside, the sequence of violent and frenzied outbursts stops abruptly. As she sleeps in her bed Othello hesitates, marvels at her beauty, bends down and kisses her, and then, against what was anticipated, he starts to weep. When she wakes, he confesses that he has come to kill her and tells her to pray; and when she does pray – 'heaven / Have mercy on me' – he answers by praying with her, 'Amen, with all my heart' (V.ii.34–5). Only when she sees hope that he will not kill her, does this new gentleness vanish, and physical instincts again take over. He utters a sound which is no word at all (l. 39) and she sees a 'bloody passion' in the gnawing of his nether lip and the shaking of his 'very frame' (ll. 40–1, 46–8). With Othello still hesitating to act and both speaking of the stolen handkerchief, their pauses, assertions, and one-word questions and answers indicate an intense struggle to grasp what is happening, as both are emotionally and physically incapable of sustained speech. Only when she seems to weep for Cassio's death, does Othello act with the unrestrained violence that the audience has repeatedly been led to expect, although, even now, it is without the decisive suddenness he had anticipated before entering the bedchamber. Several lines after 'Down, strumpet!' and 'Nay, an you strive' (ll. 83, 85), Othello silences Desdemona and, as the stage direction says, '*Smothers her*'.[14]

This is the only time that Shakespeare required a woman to be deliberately and gradually killed on stage. The shock and pain must have stunned audiences unprepared for such a scene, even though earlier uncontrollable actions had led them to expect that Othello would kill brutally and compulsively. Why should Othello take the time to smother her when he had intended to act swiftly and stain her bed with blood (see V.i.36)? By the end of the scene it has been revealed that on his person or hidden in the bedroom three weapons have been secreted, any one of which could have done the lethal work quickly. In performance it can seem that Othello is compelled to kill his wife in this slow and deliberate way because he is afraid to 'scar that whiter skin of hers than snow, /And smooth as monumental alabaster' (V.ii.4–5). In other performances, having at last come to the moment for action, his savage violence has been appeased or spent and a sexual necessity draws him to be physically close to her body. The sequence of violently physical reactions ensures that the slow and deliberate killing comes against expectation and that the actor will carry out the murder in whatever way he is led by the progress of the performance, until this moment, leads him. Emilia is '*at the door*' and calls before Desdemona is quite dead, yet Othello continues to kill her, until he utters a simple repetition, 'So, so' (l. 92).[15] For each performance the actor will discover whether this is spoken brutally or in satisfaction, relief, or exhaustion.

The repeated attempts to kill Desdemona are appallingly slow to take effect and the impression they make on the audience is heightened by a stumbling inadequacy of speech. When Emilia enters the room, Desdemona revives and speaks again, still very simply but now unambiguously shielding her husband from the consequences of his crime:

DESDEMONA   A guiltless death I die.
EMILIA   O, who hath done this deed?
DESDEMONA   Nobody. I myself. Farewell.
　　　Commend me to my kind lord. O, farewell!

Later, realizing that Iago has duped him and that his wife was innocent, Othello lies down and roars (see ll. 200), an action that repeats, in a very different context and manner, his falling on the floor in a helpless trance.

Later, after a torrent of words, he lets out a sustained, repetitive, and culminating cry: 'O Desdemona! Dead! Desdemona! Dead! O! O!' (l. 284–5). Finally, he again speaks at length to give a public account of his entire life and then suddenly, with a weapon no one thought he possessed, he kills himself, and at the last moment, turns to Desdemona:

> I kiss'd thee ere I kill'd thee. No way but this –
> Killing my self, to die upon a kiss.

By these few words and a deliberate physical action Shakespeare was able to combine the bare horror of a self-inflicted death with a renewed assertion of that gentle love and quiet deliberation that, against expectation, had taken hold of his mind and body when he approached his wife to kill her.

Repetition with difference is everywhere in all forms of art, defining what is presented and developing reception. In music, lyric poetry, painting, or architecture its presence and effectiveness are obvious to any listener, reader, or viewer, but, in theatre, spatial and visual repetitions achieve their full power only in performance and a reader of play-texts needs to take care to avoid missing or undervaluing their choreographic and cumulative effects.

* * *

Entries and exits, repeated actions and changing spatial relationships from scene to scene are all means of controlling stage action that leave their marks in a play-text. Many more temporary or limited choreographic devices are also visible, the most obvious being changes of costume that introduce new stage business and behaviour. The male disguise of heroines in the comedies alters their physical performance, precedence in encounters, and confidence in movement. When an actor puts on armour or carries a sword his timing, physical awareness, and distance from others are all affected. In Shakespeare's day especially, the clothes for travel were more protective and restricting than those worn indoors, clothes for formal occasions far richer than those for private life or outdoors activities. The significance of dress is illustrated in an episode made familiar by two widely circulated film versions: King Henry the Fifth borrows a cloak to hide his royal insignia when he wishes to behave, outwardly, like an unremarkable man. The all-powerful monarch can then be polite to the boastful Pistol, stand by to watch as two captains quarrel, and listen patiently when contradicted by a small group of footsoldiers. A change from verse to prose accompanies this change in posture, attention, and, to some degree, security, which encourages an audience to see the play's hero in a new light. And here he can be out of focus while others hold attention confidently.

A still more striking and sudden choreographic change occurs in *Henry IV, Part Two* when the actor who was Prince Hal enters in his coronation robes as King Henry the Fifth. Falstaff hails him with 'God save thee, my sweet boy!' but the only reply is addressed to the Lord Chief Justice, asking him to deal with 'that vain man'. When this official fails to staunch his old friend's fervour, the new king halts in his progress and assumes a distanced and dismissive authority:

FALSTAFF   My King! My Jove! I speak to thee, my heart!
KING   I know thee not, old man. Fall to thy prayers.
(V.v.47–8)

But the royal personage does not prove to be completely in control of himself: his posture will change as he does remember the past they once shared and his part in it. Only after he has confessed his own short-comings does Henry resume full authority: he moves on, breaking off contact and ordering the Lord Justice to act on his behalf. When this representative of the king returns with Officers shortly afterwards, Falstaff and his company are summarily sent to prison. Falstaff has been given no verbal reply to Henry's repudiation and none is needed because the change in physical behaviour will show visually at how great a mutual cost the transformation has been achieved. While King Henry's words delineate the political and intellectual content of the drama, what Falstaff identifies as the 'heart' of their relationship is expressed through performance and choreography: how the actors speak their lines and their contrasted postures, their distance from each other, the timing and size of their movements, the ways in which they look at each other or turn away.

Costumes when especially assumed for making an entrance or carrying out specified actions are a resource that Shakespeare used frequently to control and emphasize physical performance. In *The Tragedy of Coriolanus* the hero changes clothes and behaviour repeatedly. For his first entrance in the first scene, he is a young Roman nobleman, who meets an elderly friend among a crowd of plebeian citizens and then is found by a number of experienced Generals, Senators, and elected politicians, who bring urgent news that demands his response: each of these meetings calls for different behaviour. Rome is at war with invading Volscians when he next appears, and he has become a soldier among soldiers: stage directions require him to enter '*cursing*'[16] (I.iv.29, SD). In the fighting that follows, he enters the gates of Corioli alone and, almost at once, returns to the stage '*bleeding*' (l. 63, SD); he then leaves again for renewed fighting along with reinforcements. After further engagements, at the start of the ninth scene of the first Act, he enters with '*his arm in a scarf*' and leaves at its end to wash off the blood that is drying and 'should be look'd to' (ll. 93–4). The action moves back to Rome for Act II and starts by building expectation for a hero's entry, with Coriolanus at the centre of a military triumph, his brows '*crown'd with an oaken garland*', but then, against expectation, he '*kneels*' to his mother, who at once orders him to stand (l. 162). For Act II, scene ii, he is the reluctant and ill-at-ease soldier at a formal meeting of the Senate, where he is chosen as candidate for Consul. Consequently, he next appears '*in*

a gown of humility' in order to petition the plebeians for
their votes, as custom insisted; he should also show his
wounds, but to that he does not agree.

Now Coriolanus visibly alternates between the politi-
cian and the private man until he is surrounded by '*a
rabble of Plebeians*': he '*draws his sword*' and challenges
them to 'try upon [them]selves' what they (and the audience) have seen him do on the field of battle
(III.i.223–5). At the start of Act IV, when he is a banished
man and about to leave Rome, a stage direction specifies
an entrance '*with the young Nobility of Rome*' and then, in
its fourth scene, located in the enemy city of Antium, he
must enter alone, '*in mean apparel, disguised and muffled*'.
Throughout the rest of the play, Coriolanus is dressed, as
the highest ranking General, in clothes and armour that
will have been supplied by the Volscians. He has become
a marked renegade at a time when a soldier's safety in
battle depended on the heraldic colours and distinctive
clothing that demonstrated his allegiance. Almost all the
time, however, his presence remains both impressive and
dangerous. Cominius, who has been sent to negotiate
peace, reports how he had knelt to his former comrade:
'I tell you he does sit in gold, his eye / Red as 'twould
burn Rome' (V.i.63–4). Coriolanus's behaviour changes
when his mother is about to leave, having come with
others to beg and kneel for peace. Here the Folio text
directs '*He holds her by the hand, silent*' and still more re-
markably, as his words subsequently make clear, he starts
to weep: 'it is no little thing', he says, 'to make / Mine
eyes to sweat compassion' (V.iii.195–6). In the last
moments of the tragedy, Aufidius, his Volscian opposite,
recalls this moment in more sensational terms:

> He whin'd and roar'd away your victory,
> That pages blush'd at him, and men of heart
> Look'd wond'ring each at others.
>
> (V.vi.98–100)

When Aufidius continues and calls him 'thou boy of
tears' (V.vi.101), this insult enrages him more than

being branded a traitor. Repeating the offensive 'Boy!', Coriolanus provokes the assassination that had been already planned, and which is now carried out ignominiously. In common with other tragic heroes, Coriolanus is last seen as a dead body, but the manner in which he reaches this end is exceptional, the conclusion of a long sequence of variously costumed and carefully choreographed appearances.

* * *

To understand the wide range of Shakespeare's achievements, a reader must keep the space of the stage in mind, and the physical reality, movements, and activities of everyone present. This visible and tangible drama does not always leap off the page but it invariably signifies, alongside the words of dialogue and, sometimes, to a greater or contrary effect. It has the advantage of speaking directly to the senses and so registering in an audience's consciousness without having to be verbally described or understood. The effect of this choreography can be broad or overwhelming when created by a shouting, marching, dancing, or singing crowd, and intimate and specific when a single person makes a new entry or awakens to a new perception or purpose. Once a reader becomes aware of what is happening on stage, as well as what is being said, Shakespeare's invention and imagination is seen to be as fully engaged in the use of space and directions for the actors' physical performance as it is, more obviously, in his choice and management of words.

Notes

1. See Introduction, pp. 2–4, above, Chapter 1, pp. 23–4, and Chapter 2, pp. 44–7 and 48–52.
2. See, pp. 43–4 and 48–9, above.
3. See Chapter 8, pp, 171–3, below.
4. See V.iii.24–6 and V.v.19–28.
5. See *Romeo and Juliet, Twelfth Night,* and *Measure for Measure.*
6. The Folio's stage direction says that the Witches enter '*meeting* Hecate'. She may have been 'flown' on stage from above on some form of stage machinery. Before she leaves she says that 'I am for th' air' and that her 'little spirit ... / Sits in a foggy cloud, and stays for me' (III.v.20 and 34–5).
7. *A Midsummer Night's Dream,* III.ii.100–1; *The Tempest,* V.i.276; III.iii.104–9; V.i.7–19 and 56, SD.
8. Scholars have cast doubts on the authenticity of all that relates to Hecate, and certainly Thomas Middleton wrote the songs that are quoted in the Folio text. If someone other than Shakespeare wrote Hecate's long speech, he would have seen the power and significance of the Witches' physical performance elsewhere in the play and could have assumed its continuance here.
9. See above, p. 59.
10. Rudolph Arnheim, *The Power of the Center: A Study of Composition in the Visual Arts* (Berkeley, CA: University of California, 1988).
11. The scenes are: I.ii, III.ii, and V.ii.
12. Arnheim, *The Power of the Center,* pp. 21–2.
13. Ibid., p. 22.
14. So the Folio text; the Quarto's '*he stifles her*' may indicate a more violent act. While neither verb implies a swift action, both imply the use of implacable force that would draw him very close to his victim.
15. For the occurrence of such simple speech at a crucial moment, see Chapter 3, p. 73, above.
16. Editors generally agree that the Folio text of 1623 was set from a manuscript close to Shakespeare's autograph and that its stage directions are more than usually authoritative; see R. B. Parker's edition (Oxford: Oxford University Press, 1994), pp. 138–9.

5

Awakening the Senses:
an Actor's Task

The methods of training and rehearsal that actors are familiar with today were unknown in Shakespeare's day. Stanislavski's use of specific emotional memories and Brecht's questioning, dialectical concern with history and politics were unimaginable: the vocabulary they used and their self-awareness were unavailable. Equally, 'theatre games' were not played and individually expressive movement was not encouraged as a means of exploring the use of space and developing a student's creativity.[1] No one had been to an acting school or attended workshops given by masters of the art; acting was learnt by apprenticeship and by taking small roles within a company. Most modern facilities and facilitators have to be left out of the account if we want to know how Shakespeare expected his actors to respond to the texts, sustaining long roles and respecting the subtleties and innovations that are found on almost every page.

Already in this book some assumptions about performance have been made based on documents and details of the play-texts. When Shakespeare wrote he was constantly provoking an actor's imagination, varying his demands from scene to scene and within a single speech. At the same time, he would give instructions about physical performance, where to move, how to move, with whom to make contact, and much else that had to be done. These matters have already been discussed but wider implications for theatre practice have been left to this chapter: how did actors contribute to a theatrical event and by what means did they 'present' the persons they played?

* * *

In order to respond to the detailed demands of the texts, an actor's mind, imagination, and every physical faculty have to be ready to function and this involves the senses and muscles as well as cognitive and verbalized thought.[2] Consequently, every role will be played according to the individual physique, intelligence, sensibility, life-story, and theatrical experience of the performer. No two actors are the same in these respects, and therefore they can never give the same performance. And no performance will be constant from day to day as the actor's immediate circumstances, mood, and mind-set are bound to change, and as he or she responds to different audiences. Because these ingredients are always changing, there can be no such thing as an authoritative or definitive interpretation of a role, still less of an entire play. Shakespeare himself could not have foreseen how his words would come to life on any particular day.

The one constant ingredient from performance to performance and for all readers is the play-text. In most cases its words will be close to those that Shakespeare wrote, allowing for the changes, usually quite small though sometimes very significant, that have been caused by accident or introduced from time to time by scribe, editor, printer, book-keeper, stage-manager, actor, or director. While response to the words varies and is always unstable, the words, once printed, are fixed and unchanging, not only in themselves but also in their relationship to each other. Verse-lining and occasional rhymes, the size and shape of sentences in both prose and verse, and the control that syntax exercises on phrasing and emphasis are other fixed elements of the text and their effect is far more constant in performance.

Shakespeare did not follow rules of metre inflexibly but if actors respect them when phrasing speech and giving emphasis, performance gains a degree of stability and authority that it lacks in other respects. Syntax provides a still more constant and unequivocal element because an actor will not communicate the sense of a text unless the main verbs and the subjects of sentences have been identified and given their due prominence.

An actor's attention to syntax is especially necessary to bring order and clarity to the long and complex sentences that are commonly found in plays written for Elizabethan theatres. Because Latin was taught in grammar schools and translation to and from that inflected language was used to improve a student's writing in English, more attention was paid to syntax than is common in education today and the effect of this became instinctive for writers and percolated down to educated readers and thoughtful speakers. Add a respect for the rhetorical figures of speech that were used in training for oratory, legal argument and other forms of persuasion, especially those that involved repetition and balance, and a basis has been laid for writing stage dialogue that in performance has precision and gives an ongoing impression of authority.

While the effectiveness and force of words will vary with each actor's intelligence, imagination, and delivery and with the response of individual members of an audience, the dialogue's metre, its syntax, and the shape of its sentences are more constant from one performance to another, given actors with appropriate skills. Being largely aural, these elements can operate secretly, without conveying any verbalized meaning at all. They speak directly to the senses as music does and, as was frequently said of Orpheus,[3] they are able to influence the most uneducated and unreasonable of audiences. For these reasons, any study of a play in performance should, at some stage, pay attention to this sensuous, subtly attractive, and occasionally discordant element. This is what, consciously or unconsciously, every actor and every spectator does. For example, take time to consider phrase by phrase how Claudius attempts to pray, in *Hamlet*, Act III, scene iii:

> O, my offence is rank, it smells to heaven;
> It hath the primal eldest curse upon't –
> A brother's murder! Pray can I not,
> Though inclination be as sharp as will.
> My stronger guilt defeats my strong intent,
> And like a man to double business bound,
> I stand in pause where I shall first begin,
> And both neglect. What if this cursed hand
> Were thicker than itself with brother's blood,
> Is there not rain enough in the sweet heavens
> To wash it white as snow? Whereto serves mercy
> But to confront the visage of offence?
> And what's in prayer but this twofold force,
> To be forestalled ere we come to fall,
> Or pardon'd being down? Then I'll look up;
> My fault is past. But, O, what form of prayer
> Can serve my turn? 'Forgive me my foul murder'!
> That cannot be; since I am still possess'd ...
>
> (ll. 36ff.)

The words are not difficult to comprehend but the soliloquy and subsequent prayer come as an almost total surprise. Claudius has said nothing like this before: the repetition of *prayer* and *offence* within a few lines and, for the very first time, the use of *repent* and *repentance, curse* and *cursed, guilt* and *mercy*. '*The Mousetrap*' and Hamlet's anticipation of the murder about to be performed had only caused Claudius to call for lights and leave the stage, and that was after a silence in which he had risen to his feet. At the start of the following scene, the next time he is on stage, he still does not, or cannot, speak of his guilt except in so far as he recognizes the danger presented by Hamlet and is taking steps to send him 'speedily' out of Denmark. Guilt may well motivate some of his words and actions that come a long time before this soliloquy: for example, his reference to Cain murdering his brother Abel – 'the first corse' – which is barely relevant to his

talk with Hamlet in Act I, scene ii (l. 105). But now that
he is alone, all such intimations are eclipsed and earlier
reserve goes. After an exclamation, he speaks outright of
his 'rank' offence that 'smells to heaven'. The sudden
eruption of this thought into speech and its compact
shaping in a number of short phrases require an unusual
and strong dynamic in speech and consequently in physical performance. Aurally and visually, an audience's
attention is alerted.

The unexpected and striking transition can be made
in many ways. What kind of sound is the 'O' and does it
express pain, frustration, guilt, panic, determination, or
sober certainty? The exclamation can have no precise
meaning but expresses a non-verbalized committal to the
moment and is the vehicle for feeling and sensation. How
weighty, slow, or rapid will be the words that immediately
follow and are these addressed to the audience, to
himself, or to 'heaven'? Why is a single basic idea expressed in three self-contained phrases? Is 'it smells to
heaven' or the reference to Cain the start of a new sentence?[4] What happens physically to Claudius as he
speaks? The actor will have to carry belief in such a way
that this unusual moment follows, and derives from, his
performance earlier in the play. Then, after his first train
of thought is completed with 'a brother's murder',
Claudius's mind jumps to its consequences, his first word
being the monosyllabic verb 'Pray'. This is used in a nega-
tive construction but, being out of usual word order, it
carries an emphasis that can seem to reach to the heart
of his concern. Phrasing then lengthens and is sharpened
by antitheses, the last completed at the start of a new line,
with another short phrase – 'and both neglect' – coming
this time at its conclusion. Three questions follow, the
first accompanied by a gesture and carrying two extended visual and tactile images, the first of blood thick
on the speaker's hand, the second of rain that might
wash that hand as pure and white as snow. Next come
images of physical struggle and falling that lead to an intention to 'look up' and the consequent 'My fault is past',
both short-phrased, lightly iambic, and emphatic. This

time, however, assertion leads only to contradiction and denial, dismissing the brief thought of forgiveness. Then, once more, the speaker's mind has a longer reach.

If the actor respects the form of the language, this crisis will be compellingly spoken and the audience will hear Claudius being strong, supple, and active in mind, determined on action and yet very aware of alternative decisions, using words that suggest physical action and re-action. The guidance given by the choice and ordering of words does not solve all the actor's practical problems of performance or interpretation. Rather, it supports one dynamic that will grip attention and sharpen awareness of the speaker's internal tension and unease. It also influences the physical and sensuous nature of perfor-mance, insisting, for example, that Claudius looks at his own hand and, at that time, imagines the spilling of blood before he speaks of what forgiveness and repen-tance would require. Taking the hint of the soliloquy's first line, he may sense how that blood 'smells'.

The contrasting strength of the epithet 'sweet' and the visually strong images of washing and snow become clearer later in the soliloquy, where the shape of a sen-tence and ordering of words, if respected by the actor, will again mould or, as we might say today, direct perfor-mance. A final emphasis will be drawn to the unexpected image of 'a new-born babe', which emerges from another sequence of short phrases, this time suggesting a mental turmoil that is bound up with darkness and death, physi-cal effort and resistance. The start of each of these phrases is marked by a non-verbal exclamation:

> O wretched state! O bosom black as death!
> O limed soul, that, struggling to be free,
> Art more engag'd! Help, angels. Make assay:
> Bow, stubborn knees; and, heart, with strings of steel,
> Be soft as sinews of the new-born babe.
>
> (ll. 67–71)

Literary study of the text can appreciate this remark-able sequence of images and the varying mental energy of the writing in ways that would be too subtle and time-consuming for an audience in a theatre. An actor also can absorb these details in rehearsal and experiment with speech and action but this also is too subtle and uncommitted to be suitable for performance. When the play reaches an audience, the shape and dynamic of the writing will provide a shaping and more constant effect while the sensations aroused by the words in the actor's mind and body, alternately bracing and relaxing, will communicate to all members of an audience without conscious apprehension. The music of speech and the actor's varying sensations in performance are sufficient to hold an audience's attention and it is this shared sense-experience that will direct how Claudius's next words are spoken and heard: 'All may be well.' How much hope these words should carry is not indicated by Shakespeare's choice of words; they are too simple for that. Nor do they tell the actor how long the king remains kneeling afterwards, how he kneels and how still he remains, how deeply he breathes, what the following silence communicates to an audience. Hamlet, entering at this moment and perhaps hearing the last words of the soliloquy, assumes that the prayer is effective, and only later does Claudius say that it is not:

> My words fly up, my thoughts remain below.
> Words without thoughts never to heaven go.

The effect of this soliloquy is not defined in words or limited by them because some thoughts remain without words and because its most constant elements are syntax and metre. What it achieves in performance depends, more than anything else, on the sense impressions that each actor creates afresh with each playing of the scene; to these any member of any audience instinctively will respond.[5]

* * *

Verse, syntax, and the shape of sentences are reliable elements in the music of speech and help to direct the dance of performance. Many of the passages already considered illustrate this. When Beatrice speaks in soliloquy after being tricked into believing that Benedick is in love with her (see p. 105, above), rhymed iambics march forward confidently until the concluding couplet when the music changes. At the end of its first line is placed a first-person personal pronoun, 'I', which is the beginning of a new phrase; its second line starts strongly with a verb in the indicative tense but finishes with an adverb, is used comparatively, and which is the soliloquy's only word of four syllables, three of them being light front vowels:

> If thou dost love, my kindness shall incite thee
> To bind our loves up in a holy band;
> For others say thou dost deserve, and I
> Believe it better than reportingly.   *Exit.*
> (*Much Ado About Nothing*, III.i.113–16)

With a new resolve to love Benedick, the performer might wish to finish the soliloquy and the scene by standing firmly centre-stage but the lightness and metrically displaced emphases of the last couplet direct otherwise. Beatrice may linger on stage, for a brief moment, doubtful once more, or she might run off stage as she says the last words, eager to catch sight of him.

When Macbeth returns from re-visiting the corpses of the king and two grooms whom he has killed, and must face the assembled Thanes (see above, p. 95), the phrasing of his speech suggests a stillness in which the mind ranges widely and words are unforced. At first he only alludes to what he has seen, his thoughts turning to his own death and a 'blessed time' that is now passed. Then, changing tack again on 'for', he explains why he has spoken in this way, using general terms and then, very briefly, a metaphor – 'All is but toys.' Finally, speech moves again to generality and back to metaphor, in two phases this time, the second more extended and in two stages that conclude by evoking a vision of vast size and implication:

> Had I but died an hour before this chance,
> I had liv'd a blessed time; for, from this instant,
> There's nothing serious in mortality –
> All is but toys; renown and grace is dead;
> The wine of life is drawn, and the mere lees
> Is left this vault to brag of.

(II.iii.89–94)

With 'lees' the sense of taste is drawn into the visual imagery, and the verb 'brag', strongly placed at the end of a sentence, adds an active element. Before the end of the play, Macbeth will be more strongly haunted by the vision of a 'blessed time' that has been forfeited: then he will enumerate the 'honour, love, obedience, troops of friends' he has lost and recognize that the a life-time's effort will signify 'nothing' (V.iii.24–7 and V.v.28). The shape and sounds of his short speech after the public discovery of the murder, together with its varying imagery, establish an aural and sensuous dynamic that gives scope for expression of Macbeth's deepest feelings at a time when everyone on stage is tense in expectation of more information about the murder.

In scenes with many persons on stage, the shaping of one person's speech often has wide physical repercussions. Taking another earlier example, when Gertrude calms Hamlet at Ophelia's graveside (see pp. 83–4, above), a very short speech – 'O my son, what theme?' (V.i.262) – carries enough energy to stop his struggle with Laertes and a number of attendants. The double thrust of the exclamatory and personal appeal, followed by a crucial and direct question, has sufficient force to elicit the unprecedented openness and simplicity of 'I loved Ophelia.' A little later, when Hamlet has attacked Laertes with words rather than physical strength, Gertrude calms him to another surprising effect, at first by completing his verse-line with alliterative emphasis and then, once she has

gained attention, by embarking on a far-fetched and sensitive simile that extends over two and a half lines:

> HAMLET   … an thou'lt mouth,
> I'll rant as well as thou.
> QUEEN   This is mere madness;
> And thus awhile the fit will work on him;
> Anon, as patient as the female dove
> When that her golden couplets are disclos'd,
> His silence will sit drooping.
> HAMLET   Hear you, sir:
> What is the reason that you use me thus?
> I lov'd you ever… .
>
> (V.i.277–84)

In various individual ways, every other actor on stage,
from the one who plays the king to those who are nameless attendants, will have to accommodate their performances to the timing, shape, and gentle rhythm of
Gertrude's words. By this means, Shakespeare has
ensured that the renewed sympathy between mother and
son makes a physical and sensuous effect, and therefore
one that is unambiguous and more constant than others
from performance to performance.

All such details of verse, syntax, and phrasing are commonly the object of literary studies but to understand a
play in performance the speakers and others on stage
with them have to be taken into account at the same time,
not only as minds that think and speak but, rather, as
complete human beings. While Shakespeare was writing
the dialogue, the persons of the drama were physically
present in his imagination – breathing, moving, energized, and potentially alive in all their senses – and he
knew that these fictional persons would be created on
stage by actors whose actual presence would be, for an audience, a principal feature of their experience of the play,
quite possibly the dominant and most lasting one.[6] The
task for theatrical study is to understand the play-text in a
similar manner, asking what guidance to actors has been
written into the shape and sound of the speeches and

what will be an audience's response to the sensuous qualities of performance.

* * *

When sense-experience is taken into account, study of a play-text enters territory with boundless possibilities and comparatively little certainty. Opportunities to awaken the senses are everywhere and can lead in divergent directions. The verbal calls for sensuous awareness in the acting of Hamlet's most famous soliloquy (see p. 2, above) are so varied and so numerous that to follow each and every one, thoroughly and from moment to moment, would be a very demanding task and take a long time in both rehearsal and performance. It would probably confuse an audience by obscuring narrative progress. In practice, actors make a choice between the many possibilities of enactment and develop their own course through the text's various and numerous cues for sense-response, action, and vocal expression. The result is that no two performances are the same. Almost every passage of a few lines that has been considered in this book could awaken a number of different sensations, some of passing or simple effect, others complex or mysterious in origin; some are in conflict with each other, like the 'thick-coming fancies' that keep Lady Macbeth from her rest (see pp. 44–7, above).

While we cannot know how responsive Elizabethan actors were to a text's subtleties and fine distinctions or how conscious they were of making choices, a considerable number of plays have survived that challenge actors in this way. What we cannot doubt is that acting in Shakespeare's day drew upon the senses as well as upon thought, and that, on occasion, it was sensational in effect. We have Polonius's word that the First Player in *Hamlet* 'turn'd his colour, and ha[d] tears in 's eyes' by the time he had concluded a speech that was written with modesty and cunning; later Hamlet says that the actor's 'whole function' had suited 'with forms to his conceit'.

In mid-performance one phrase, 'the mobled queen', so awakens Hamlet's own imagination that he instinctively repeats it, interrupting the performance (II.ii.512–13, 496, and 549–50). Turning from this very special case to consider 'bully Bottom', the popular non-professional actor, we find he is very aware of the need to awaken the senses. He is confident that he can 'move storms' and shed tears on demand; he also boasts of being able to 'condole' in a 'monstrous little voice' (*A Midsummer Night's Dream*, I.ii.16–46). The most comprehensive description of acting in Shakespeare's plays is in *Richard the Third*, when the dukes of Gloucester and Buckingham discuss how they will give the impression that they are afraid, and the kingdom in danger:

> GLOUCESTER   Come, cousin, canst thou quake and
> change thy colour,
>   Murder thy breath in middle of a word,
>   And then again begin, and stop again,
>   As if thou were distraught and mad with terror?
> BUCKINGHAM   Tut, I can counterfeit the deep tragedian;
>   Speak and look back, and pry on every side,
>   Tremble and start at wagging of a straw,
>   Intending deep suspicion. Ghastly looks
>   Are at my service, like enforced smiles;
>   And both are ready in their offices
>   At any time to grace my stratagems.
>
> (III.v.1–11)

The expectation is that actors exercise physical control over performance and can demonstrate emotion and sentiment solely by breathing, timing, and impulsive actions. By these physical and aural means, feelings will seem to originate from 'deep' within, and convince an audience by their seeming reality.

Besides occasional descriptions of performance, there are many more of behaviour that arises from fear, anger, love, and other feelings that are expressed by action and not words. Ophelia's description of Hamlet's off-stage entrance to her closet implies bearing and actions that are instinctive rather than rational; if he was only pretending to 'assume' a mad disposition, his acting involved touch, sight, breathing, nervous tension, muscle, and blood-flow to the face, so that sensations arising from madness seemed to be truly felt. She reports that he came before her:

> ... with his doublet all unbrac'd,
> No hat upon his head, his stockings fouled,
> Ungart'red and down-gyved to his ankle;
> Pale as his shirt, his knees knocking each other,
> And with a look so piteous in purport
> As if he had been loosed out of hell
> To speak of horrors ...
>
> (II.i.78–84)

On stage at other times Hamlet is required to be similarly wrought on both lesser and greater occasions: when seeing his father's Ghost, 'every petty arture' [*artery* or *sinew*] is made 'as hardy as the Nemean Lion's nerve'; having walked in a lobby alone for up to four hours, 'sadly the poor wretch comes reading'; duelling for his life, he becomes 'incensed' (I. iv.82–3; II.ii.159–60, 167; and V.ii.295).

In the comedies, Malvolio is said to be transformed into 'a rare turkey-cock ... [as] he jets under his advanc'd plumes'; Hermia is seen to 'quake with fear' and the next moment 'almost' swoons as she leaves the stage; Rosalind promises to 'weep for nothing' or 'laugh like a hyen[a]' and, being unable to 'be out of the sight of Orlando', she leaves the stage to 'go find a shadow, and sigh till he come'.[7] As well as the imagination, sense-reactions must be alert and strong if all this is to carry conviction in performance. Mindless instinct should, at times, seem to dictate or subvert what a person intends to do or say, and its effect ought to be evident in a moment. Speaking the words of Shakespeare's text is insufficient in performance without an actor's entire sensibility being involved and outwardly expressed in physical performance. In study of his plays, a reader's task is to respond in a similarly sensuous manner.

* * *

When studying the plays, both actors and readers can find so many possible readings that, to avoid being overwhelmed, they tend to choose only a few for close attention. This process of selection is helpful because, beneath the varying impulses and conflicting intentions found in a single major role, one more permanent inclination or appetite can often be identified, a single instinct, disposition, sensation or sentiment that is present throughout the play. This core involves sense-reactions and instincts rather than verbalized thought: it is a distinctive quality of being that exists in the body or at some scarcely conscious level of the mind; and it is ongoing, whatever is happening on stage or whatever is being said. The persons in Shakespeare's plays are not provided with the kind of recognizable individuality that would derive from a detailed biography nor do they often possess a specific physical constitution. They are not, in a word, what would today be called 'characters'. Their 'quality of being' is not so restrictive because, within the basis this offers for performance, other impulses, feelings, and sensations can freely arise and momentarily affect action and speech. Once recognized it provides a magnetic point whereby an actor can find direction and activate all the senses. By the same means, study will gain a clearer understanding of the structure of a play and the progressive experience of its audiences.[8]

Some of Shakespeare's *dramatis personae* have been given names that identify just such a core temperament. The type characters of Roman comedy had established a tradition that is partly responsible for Parolles, who is too talkative for his own good, and for Sir Toby Belch, given to improprieties, Touchstone, quick with opinion, Le Beau, practised as a courtier, or Borachio, given to drinking (from the Spanish *borracho*). Some plays have many persons named in this way: *Henry the Fourth, Part II* has Pistol, Shallow, Silence, Mouldy, Shadow, Wart, Feeble, Bullcalf, Fang, Snare, Mistress Quickly and Doll Tearsheet. *A Midsummer Night's Dream* has a group of them:

Quince, Snug, Bottom, Flute, Snout, and Starveling. Persons taken from history sometimes live up to their names in much the same way: Hotspur is quick and fiery in action, Fortinbras, strong-armed in action. Sir John Falstaff is a more complicated example: while his physical and sexual vigour is evidently 'falling', his intentions and imagination are often amazingly resilient. Another clearly ambiguous name is Angelo in *Measure for Measure*, who proves to be 'angel'' only 'on the outward side' (III.ii.254). Even the most apt of these names are sometimes contravened as a play gains momentum; for example, Silence eventually breaks into song in celebration of a merry heart so that Falstaff declares, 'I did not think Master Silence had been a man of this mettle' (*Henry IV, Part Two*, V.iii.37–8).

Around the end of the sixteenth century, it became fashionable to call such a simple attribute a 'humour'. Ben Jonson gave a new currency to this medieval medical term with the title of his comedy, *Every Man in His Humour* (1598). A sequel soon followed *Every Man Out of His Humour* (1599), with an Induction in which Asper explains that a humour is a 'general disposition':

> As when some one peculiar quality
> Doth so possess a man, that it doth draw
> All his affects, his spirits, and his powers,
> In their confluxions, all to run one way... .

This is very much its meaning in Shakespeare's comedies and histories written around the same time, where the word is used to identifiy a person's distinctive or core quality. In *Much Ado About Nothing* (1598–9), when Benedick boasts that 'a college of wit-crackers cannot flout me out of my humour' he means that his nature is such that he will always think his own thoughts and say what he thinks (V.iv.99–101). In *Julius Caesar* (1599), Brutus complains that a choleric Cassius expects him to 'stand and crouch / Under your testy humour' and, a little later, Cassius admits that the 'rash humour which my mother gave me / Makes me forgetful,' meaning that this is an indelible part of himself that draws all that he does 'to run one way' (IV.iii.45–6 and 118–19). In *Henry the Fifth* and *The Merry Wives of Windsor*, both written at about this time, the word becomes a joke when Corporal Nym uses it repeatedly to assert that he is a man whose will cannot be crossed with impunity. Even without using the word, the assumption underlying Jonson's definition is frequently to be found in the plays. Linking his courage to his 'choler', which was a specific humour in the medieval medical sense, King Henry makes a moral judgement on Fluellen's 'one peculiar quality' and is very sure what will happen next:

> ... I do know Fluellen valiant,
> And touch'd with choler, hot as gunpowder,
> And quickly will return an injury.
>
> (*Henry V*, IV.vii.174–6)

A notable example is Malvolio, whose name, from the Italian *mala voglia*, indicates a misplaced or misused love and whose self-love is exposed by Maria from beneath his moral pretensions:

> The devil a Puritan that he is, ... the best persuaded of himself, so cramm'd, as he thinks, with excellencies that it is his grounds of faith that all that look on him love him.
>
> (*Twelfth Night*, II.iii.137–42)

Identifying a general disposition is commonly the way to understand what is happening in the plays, for example the sardonic joke about the Duke of Gloucester, later Richard the Third, 'He 's sudden, if a thing comes in his head' (*Henry VI, Part Three*, V.v.86).

In leading roles a basic and 'peculiar' quality of being is seldom identified or made manifest so clearly as in these examples but, if an actor, director, or student searches in the text for evidence, it will nearly always be found. Often several will be plausible and sometimes it seems that Shakespeare purposefully introduced a number of contrary clues in order to puzzle an audience and provoke close attention. Hamlet is a notorious example. He is the 'sweet prince' with a 'noble heart' who is greatly loved 'by the general gender'. Even Claudius recognizes that he is 'Most generous, and free from all contriving' and Fortinbras knows that he was likely 'To have prov'd most royal' (V.ii.351; IV.vii.18 and 135; V.ii.390). And yet, considered another way, he is 'dangerous' and capable of 'impious stubbornness' (IV.iii.2; I.ii.94); by his own admission, he is 'very proud, revengeful, ambitious', and also a 'dull and muddy-mettl'd rascal' and 'your only jig-maker' (III.i.125–6; II.ii.561; III.ii.120). He becomes highly secretive – 'I must hold my tongue' – and defies anyone to 'pluck the out heart of [his] mystery' (I.ii.159; III.iii.357–8). From among these contrary indications, an actor can chose a basic 'quality of being' that will become progressively more apparent in performance. Similarly, a reader who chooses one for study throughout the play will build a continuous and comprehensive sense of what happens in performance and bring the text alive in the imagination. A useful rule for actor and student is to identify the quality of being that sustains the role in its very last moments, when other resources have failed or are lost to view. It is also likely to be one that strongly influences performance at those critical junctures where words fail and the actor's presence on stage is all that sustains the playing.[9]

Hamlet, it may be thought, is governed throughout the play by a sense of duty to the Danish kingdom and his royal lineage or, alternatively, by the love he feels for his mother, Ophelia, and his father, or by grief for his father's death and then for Ophelia's, or by an instinct to act and give each thought its deed, or by disgust and shame at his own faults, or by a desire for oblivion, or by a need to maintain his sanity among many contrary sensations. Any one of these continuing and instinctive feelings could lead Hamlet towards the tragedy's conclusion and yet, in that moment, another quality seems to dominate, one that has frequently been obscured by others:

Hamlet's desire for peace. The feelings and sensations arising from this instinct are present throughout the play. Immediately before the end he thinks of death as a 'felicity' (V.ii.339) and tries to bring peace to Denmark by giving his voice for settling the succession on the strong-armed Fortinbras. His dying words, 'the rest is silence', can be spoken as a contented acceptance of the 'consummation' that death will bring and he had previously 'devoutly wished for' (III.i.60–4). The same instinctive desire to be at peace has recurred in different forms throughout the play. Hamlet tells Horatio that he values him as one whose 'blood and judgment' are well 'comeddled' (III.ii.66–71). He says that his father had a god-like 'grace' and, having made peace with Gertrude, he promises to exchange his blessing with hers and five times wishes her 'good night' as if sealing their newly won accord (III.iv.55–62 and 159–217). His first response to Ophelia, before thinking of his own 'sins', is 'Soft you now! / The fair Ophelia,' as if other feelings have been arrested by her presence (III.i.88–9). When he grows violent with thoughts of betrayal, he repeatedly tells her to seek refuge in a nunnery as if that might be a safe-haven and bring her peace. From what she knows and has felt, she has no doubt that his true state of being had made 'music' of his vows and that he was unmatched in 'form and feature' (III.i.150–61). As noted earlier (see pp. 83–4), Hamlet's anger and grief are calmed at Ophelia's funeral when Gertrude speaks of a peaceful dove. He is most obviously at peace with himself and his fate immediately before the last encounters, in which he will kill and be killed: at this moment, he recognizes 'a special providence in the fall of a sparrow' and, with a simple 'Let be', is prepared to accept death whenever and however it comes (V.ii.211–17).

Hamlet's instinctive capacity for peace is also signalled by many word-choices and recurrent images. His very first puns and figures of speech are about kinship and kindness, balance, and the all-seeing sun. Agreeing to stay in Elsinore, he says more than is necessary – 'I shall in all my best obey you, madam' (I.ii.120) – as if he wishes that relationship were complete and secure. Left alone and speaking in soliloquy, he longs to 'resolve into a dew', that is, to melt and also to dispel uncertainty, and the common pun on what is *due* may also be present. His thoughts then turn to 'the Everlasting' who is 'fixed' in his demands. Disgusted at the state of the world, Hamlet immediately likens it to an 'unweeded garden', in which may be included the thought that it should be tended and ordered; then he remembers his 'excellent' father, who could make even 'the winds of heaven' less rough (I.ii.129ff.). These and many other verbal indications, occurring every time Hamlet is on stage, are of small importance in themselves but together reveal a continuous bias in his feelings even when under great and contrary pressures.

If the role is played with this permanent bias in Hamlet's nature, other sensations will find expression in a transient or secondary way; and so it would be if another core sentiment were chosen. The awakening of a number of different sense-reactions will encourage an audience to watch for a more settled and single impression which will, finally, 'denote [Hamlet] truly' (I.ii.76–86). To some extent all Shakespeare's plays are structured in this way so that the inner nature of their principal persons – the permanent bias of their beings – is progressively revealed right up until their last scene. Discovering such a basis for a play's structure and its effect on an audience's progressive experience will illuminate any study of the texts, whether in performance or on the page. Here only one more example will be briefly given because each text calls for a detailed investigation that cannot be fully presented within the bounds of this book; a scene-by-scene commentary is probably the best form of study.[10]

On early readings Rosalind in *As You Like It* might seem to be governed by a capacity for sexual and affectionate love and yet, in her last scene, she makes no reply to her bridegroom's recognition that Ganymede and Rosalind are one, and 'gives herself' in exactly the same words to both father and Orlando. Her last words in the play are to Phebe, whom she can never love. While she is obviously capable of love, her handling of Orlando when she is in disguise might suggest that laughter is her most deeply ingrained instinct and the most continuous basis for her words and actions. It would be possible to play the last scene so that Rosalind evidently enjoys her own brief words, the puzzlement of others, and the laughable neatness of it all. In rehearsal, however, it might be considered that she halts the impulse towards comedy as much as she encourages it. She speaks of laughter in a way that is not appreciative: 'I will laugh like a hyen,' she tells Orlando, 'and that when thou art inclin'd to sleep'; she reports that when she made her father laugh, he simply 'let me go' (IV.i.138–9; III.iv.31–3). Other and more frequent evidence suggests that Rosalind's most constant instinct is for action, to do or say something and not hold back. She has arranged the entire last scene of the play and takes a leading part in it and yet, when it is in action, she quickly seems to lose interest. The actor can show how Rosalind reacts to the conclusion by the way in which she takes her position beside Orlando, first at Hymen's request and then to satisfy Jaques's desire to have the last word, and finally by how she joins in the concluding dance. Then the text invites yet another demonstration of her need to take action when she comes forward to speak the Epilogue after everyone else has left.

The same bias is found throughout the comedy. Rosalind's first words are about mastering the sorrow she feels for her father's banishment and then, only a very few lines later, she proposes that they should 'devise sports' and that falling in love is to be one of them (I.ii.21–2). As she talks with Celia, her cousin, words and images are notably positive and physical: fortune is the 'cutter off of nature's wit'; Touchstone is asked to 'unmuzzle' his wisdom; Le Beau is said to enter with 'his mouth full of news' from which she expects to be 'newscrammed'. Talk of wrestling immediately interests her and it is the young and successful wrestler with whom she falls in love. Having suggested to Celia that they should leave after Orlando has won, she pretends that he has called her back, and, when he has nothing to say, she immediately takes the initiative and engages him with active words and images: 'Sir, you have wrestled well, and overthrown / More than your enemies' (I.ii.233–4).

When Rosalind woos and teases Orlando, she provides almost all the energy. Typical is her whispered aside to her cousin Celia: 'I will speak to him like a saucy lackey, and under that habit play the knave with him' (III.ii.278–80). Almost any speech can illustrate the prevalence of energetic ideas and physical images. Saying she will not have him as a lover, she piles instance on instance, all of them active:

> Troilus had his brains dash'd out with a Grecian club; yet he did what he could to die before, and he is one of the patterns of love. Leander, he would have liv'd many a fair year, though Hero had turn'd nun, if it had not been for a hot midsummer-night; for, good youth, he went but forth to wash him in the Hellespont, and, being taken with the cramp, was drown'd; ... men have died from time to time, and worms have eaten them, but not for love.
>
> (IV.i.87–94)

And so it is for much of the play, even when neither love nor laughter is her driving force: for example, to Jaques:

> Farewell, Monsieur Traveller; look you lisp and wear strange suits, disable all the benefits of your own country, be out of love with your nativity, and almost chide God for making you that countenance you are; or I will scarce think you have swam in a gondola.
>
> (IV.i.30–6)

Love, laughter, fear and, occasionally, shame, are other themes that are presented in active images. To found a performance of Rosalind or a textual interpretation of the comedy on one state of being, one core and peculiar quality, is not a severe limitation. It throws a wide range of other sensations into relief, so that they are seen more sharply with the benefit of this cross-lighting. And by changing the context in which the primary instinct operates, more of its potential is revealed, often in surprising form or to unusual effect. The sensations of a person who is active in love or in the enjoyment of laughter or in dealing with ongoing events can transform ordinary reactions and make familiar words sound fresh and unprecedented.

Placing emphasis on a permanent state of being may seem an old-fashioned way to conceive and present the individual persons in a play, lacking the finesse with which characters are treated in the prose fiction and intellectual discourse of more recent times and, to some degree, in a few earlier writings. Certainly, present-day critical studies and performances by skilled actors have shown that subtle interpretations of Shakespeare's plays can be based on quite different grounds, such as psychological processes, political and social influences, physical and sexual characteristics, or imaginary biographies and specific personal experiences. Nevertheless, judging the plays and their leading roles according to permanent states of being and the sensations they awake in performance is to follow the way in which Shakespeare conceived and presented them. This is how he felt for the persons of his plays and how he plotted the action and might be expected to assess what he had written. This is fortunate for us because sensations arising in performance are that part of a play to which any member of any audience can respond instinctively with the senses. He or she can recognize sensations that are common in daily life and respond accordingly, even though they have been transposed into a more intense illusion of life and become part of a narrative that grips and holds attention with exceptionally strong and rare feelings. While performance is inspired and informed by the details of Shakespeare's text – nothing replaces that – the effect of performance is not wholly, perhaps not chiefly, dependent on the audience's understanding of the words that are spoken. A sensory response is also involved and that is the element that enables the plays to speak beyond linguistic, ideological, or cultural boundaries.

* * *

The notion that actors should base their performances on the sensations arising from a quality of being rather than on their understanding of motives, purposes, or psychology is both ancient and modern. Lecturing at Harvard University towards the end of his career, Henry Irving said that an actor should be a student and 'put into practice the best ideas he can gather', but he added that it was his task to 'give body to those ideas – fire, force, and sensibility, without which they would remain for most people mere airy abstractions'. The actor, he said, must 'be moved by the impulse of being' – words that are close to those that have been used here, such as sensation, quality of being, 'humour', and 'individual disposition'.[11] Although Stanislavski gave student actors a great deal to think about when preparing their roles and this was later transposed into a 'system', he also insisted that 'in our art to understand is to feel'.[12] Different words may be used today but the basic notion that performance should be based on more than intellectual understanding is a commonplace in theatre training, only now the 'impulse of being' might be called 'instinct', and actors might be encouraged to 'feel' what they do by 'creative exploration'. In rehearsal 'improvisation' is often used as a key to unlock responses hidden by habit or by too much talk about the work in hand. Directors and actors use music, especially jazz, and dance, especially modern dance, to supplement what study of a play-text brings to mind.[13] But, strangely, Shakespeare's plays are often treated differently so that the actors are asked to speak the words as soon as they begin to understand them, as if speech and intellectual comprehension were the basis of performance. Priority should, rather, be given to the embodiment of the text in physical action through an imaginative assumption of the sensations, or impulse of being, appropriate to the speaker and the context.

A description of David Garrick's Hamlet, published in the 1770s, and that theatre historians have considered typical of his style of acting, shows how far an actor can rely on what is experienced by the senses – what has here been called 'sensation'. On Horatio's 'Look, my Lord, it comes':

> Garrick turns sharply, at the same time staggering back two or three steps, his knees giving way under him; his hat falls to the ground, and both his arms, the left most noticeably, are stretched out almost to their full length, his hands as high as his head, the right arm bent more with its hand lower, and the fingers apart; his mouth is open: thus he stands rooted to the spot, with legs apart, but no less of dignity, supported by his friends who are better acquainted with the apparition, and who are afraid lest he should collapse. His whole demeanour is so expressive of terror that it made my flesh creep even before he began to speak.[14]

The 'first dramatic principle' set out in Aaron Hill's *Essay on the Art of Acting* (1821) is that:

> to act a passion well, the actor never must attempt its imitation 'till his fancy has conceived so strong an image, or idea, of it as to move the same impressive springs within his mind which form that passion when 'tis undesigned and natural... .
>
> As soon as this pathetic [i.e., *moving, affecting*] sensation has strongly and fully imprinted his fancy, let him then – and never a moment before – attempt to give the speech due utterance. – So shall he always hit the right and touching sensibility of tone, and move his auditors impressingly: whereas, should he, with an unfeeling volubility of cadence, hurry on from one over-leap'd distinction to another, without due adaption of his look and muscles, to the meaning proper to the passion, he will never speak to hearts, nor move

himself nor any of his audience, beyond the simple
and unanimating verbal sense, without the *spirit* of the
writer.[15]

* * *

Any study of Shakespeare's plays will be based, naturally and se-
curely, on their texts but attention cannot so readily be given to
the sensations that arise when the plays are acted. The actual
presence of actors, how they speak and what they do, will also be
involved. Going to see performances is the first step in meeting
these demands, by opening the mind to a text's theatrical possibil-
ities, but the benefits of this will be limited. Experience and
special knowledge are needed to analyse what is witnessed on
stage and sufficiently skilled performances are not always and
everywhere available. Faced with these difficulties, students will
benefit from taking part in exploratory workshops so that they
begin to experience at first hand what happens when a text comes
alive in performance: how words and actions function together
inextricably, what sensations and feelings arise, and at what
points an audience's attention becomes especially close.[16] The
simplest practical engagement can at least start an imaginary
and sensuous involvement with performance that will aid any
study of Shakespeare's texts. Yet neither workshops nor seeing any
number of live productions is likely to provide sufficient means to
enable a reader to understand the theatrical potential of a text.
Experience in a theatre or rehearsal room needs to be supple-
mented by forms of theatrical study that can be undertaken any-
where. Detailed attention to the handling of the verse, choice of
syntax, and shaping of sentences will provide clues to what is
heard in the performance and to the actors' engagement with
defining elements in the text. Enquiry into the basic nature and
dominant sensations of the principal persons in a play – in this
chapter called their 'quality of being' and 'impulse of being' –
will clarify the structure of a play as well as the progressive expe-
rience of its audiences. Other examples of theatrical study are
found throughout this book and in other books that are
concerned with Shakespeare's plays in performance.[17]

Notes

1. Clive Barker's *Theatre Games* (London: Eyre Methuen, 1977) and the school in Paris of Jacques Lecoq have been two strong influences in this. Lecoq's methods and ways of thought have recently been made more accessible in *Jacques Lecoq and the British Theatre*, edited by Franc Chamberlain and Ralph Yarrow (London: Routledge Harwood, 2001), and Simon Murray, *Jacques Lecoq* (London: Routledge, 2003).
2. See above, pp. 2–4 and 7–9, etc.
3. See, for example, the quotation from *The Two Gentlemen of Verona* placed at the head of the Introduction, p. 1.
4. The lines are printed here following Peter Alexander's edition of 1951; the Oxford edition by G. R. Hibbard (1987) has a full stop after 'heaven', the Penguin by T. J. B. Spencer (1980) has full stops after both 'rank' and 'heaven'. The Folio of 1623 has only commas until a full stop after 'murder' (l. 38); the 'good' Quarto of 1604–5 also has all commas and another after 'murder'. The ways in which Shakespeare's text or texts were transmitted and have been edited in modern times mean that none of these ways of punctuation have Shakespeare's authority.
5. This observation is in line with the results of Professor Sauter's research and places them in a specifically Shakespearean context; see Chapter 3, pp. 74–5, above.
6. See, again, pp. 75–7, above.
7. *Twelfth Night*, II.v.28–9; *A Midsummer Night's Dream*, II.ii.148–54; *As You Like It*, IV.i.137–9, 193–5.
8. This paragraph and the subsequent argument are a development of the earlier treatment in John Russell Brown, *Shakespeare and the Theatrical Event* (Basingstoke: Palgrave Macmillan, 2002), pp. 84–95, and a paper read at a Conference on Asian Shakespeares at the University of Singapore in 2002.
9. See, again, Chapter 3, especially, pp. 70–1 and 73–4.
10. Examples of commentaries of this kind will be the main feature of a series of *Shakespeare Handbooks* that have been commissioned by Palgrave Macmillan from a number of theatrically experienced writers.
11. *The Drama: Addresses by Henry Irving* (London: Heinemann, 1893), pp. 46–7, 51.
12. Quoted from *On Stanislavsky's 'System'* (Peking: Foreign Language Press, 1969, p. 29) where his teachings are opposed to a reasoned and politically responsible art.

13. See, for example, Clive Barker, 'In Search of the Lost Mode: Improvisation and All That Jazz', *New Theatre Quarterly*, 59 (vol. xviii, Part 1), pp.10–16.

14. *Lichtenberg's Visits to England*, tr. M. L. Mare and W. H. Quarrell (Oxford: Clarendon Press, 1938), pp. 9–10.

15. Quoted from *The Works of the Late Aaron Hill*, vol. iv, second edition (London, 1854), pp. 339, 351. Interestingly, Hill distinguishes 'ten dramatic passions' that are very close to the nine basic *rasas*, or sentiments, of the Sanskrit *Natyasastra*. Hill's descriptions of movements, gestures and facial expressions appropriate for each passion are similar to those for the various *rasas* in this treatise, which is more than a thousand years old. As a young man, Hill did visit countries in the eastern Mediterranean but he would have had no access to Sanskrit manuscripts.

16. See below, pp. 201–2.

17. For an account of available studies see, for example, John Russell Brown, *Shakespeare and the Theatrical Event*, chapter 14, 'Study and Criticism'.

6

Staging the Everyday: Actual Activities

A reader of Shakespeare's plays will quickly realize that gifted and experienced actors are needed to represent the exceptional persons who speak their words and are involved in their exceptional situations and actions. Yet, at times, the words are so simple and what is happening so like the events of everyday life that no skilled performances or sophisticated staging seem to be necessary. In his own times this sense of actuality would have been more apparent than it is today because the language of the dialogue was more familiar and even its most extraordinary qualities could be recognized as a heightened form of everyday speech. Loss of verbal familiarity has far-reaching consequences because it obscures a continuous lifelikeness that the plays once possessed, a sense that everything is actually happening at the very threshold of one's own daily experience. Actors can compensate us for this loss when their sense-awareness and physical performance embody a play's action and re-animate its speeches, bringing even the most complicated speeches to palpable and present life. A reader can also resuscitate the plays by an active imagination.

Steady practice and a knowledge of Elizabethan life and language are needed to progress very far in these studies but a start can be made by identifying moments in a text that call for specific activities that continue to have an everyday familiarity, and passages with words that are so simple and so simply used that they seem as current now as they would have been in the past. One way to identify such moments is to look for speeches and incidents that would not lose very much if translated into another language. Then a reader can envisage how actual persons known in daily life would be engaged in what is happening. Or actors known from television or film can be cast as the persons of the play in one's own mind and then imagined doing what the text requires at specific moments. How quickly do these people move or how still are they? Are they alert, nervous, bold, isolated, or constantly moving? How close are they to each other as they speak or listen to the words? If a reader takes an independent initiative and allows time for patient and adventurous exploration, the texts will be surprisingly hospitable to this kind of fantasy.

* * *

King Lear is a highly complex person whether his part is read, or seen in performance, but at times he speaks only the simplest of words. The passionate conflict between the father and two daughters springs to immediately recognizable life with 'Does any here know me? This is not Lear… . Who is it that can tell me who I am?' (II.iv.225–9). All the implications will not be readily understood but the main thrust of the words is unmistakable, even on a first reading. Lear is also a king and that is not so easily considered as a present reality at this time, either on stage or in the mind of a reader. It is earlier in the play, in the formality of its very first scene, that kingship is made evident in physical expressions of anger and simply-worded assertions of authority so that, in an instant, the words of the text are entirely comprehensible:

> LEAR   … what can you say to draw
>   A third more opulent than your sisters? Speak.
> CORDELIA   Nothing, my lord.

LEAR   Nothing!
CORDELIA   Nothing.
LEAR   Nothing will come of nothing. Speak again.
CORDELIA   Unhappy that I am, I cannot heave
   My heart into my mouth... .

                    (I.i.84–91)

An understanding of what is involved at this moment will develop further during the course of the tragedy but here, at its very start, a powerful and frightening confrontation is expressed by everyday means so that, surprisingly, it can seem to be actually happening.

In one way or other the plays are seldom far from the realities of ordinary living. Few in any audience will readily identify with a king who returns from one war to find that he is threatened with another and deserted by subjects in whom he had put his trust, but, once this situation has been established, Shakespeare's Richard the Second speaks in terms to which anyone can relate:

> I live with bread like you, feel want,
> Taste grief, need friends; ...
>   (*Richard II*, III.ii.175–6)

Compact thought and the metaphoric use of *taste* guard against too facile an acceptance. In danger on the field of battle, Falstaff uses simple words in a homely phrase: 'I would 'twere bed-time, Hal, and all well.' The prince's reply, almost as simply expressed, widens the context and, for some in an audience, will imply a deeper response: 'Why, thou owest God a death' (*Henry the Fourth, Part One*, V.i.124–6). Similar examples of an unexpected shift towards timeless and everyday expression are found throughout the plays, often at crucial and deeply felt moments for example, from the comedies: 'I cannot be out of the sight of Orlando', or 'Peace; I will stop your mouth', or 'How does he love me?' In the histories and tragedies sustained speech is sometimes interrupted with simpler phrases, for example: 'What do I fear? Myself? There's none else by. / Richard loves Richard; that is, I am I', or 'I never thought to hear you speak again', or 'O Desdemona! Dead! Desdemona! Dead!'[1] Looking for plain speech, one finds it in every play and often at moments when a fundamental change takes place for the person who is speaking or in the development of the story. Everyday phrases are sometimes like strong nails driven into the fabric of the play and into the audience's consciousness, by this means becoming main features in the action, which will stay in place from one performance to another and are liable to settle in the consciousness of audiences. Or they can be thought of as doors opening onto the everyday experience and comprehension of any actor or audience member, and through which the plays are almost immediately accessible.

A sustained example is in the aftermath of Claudio and Hero's aborted wedding in *Much Ado About Nothing*. Beatrice and Benedick remain on stage after everyone else has left, and start speaking very simply:

– Lady Beatrice, have you wept all this while?
– Yea, and I will weep a while longer.
– I will not desire that.
– You have no reason; I do it freely.
– Surely I do believe your fair cousin is wronged.
– Ah, how much might the man deserve of me that would right her!

(IV.i.255ff.)

And so on for much of the encounter. Some of the words and phrases would not be used today – for example, here, 'Lady Beatrice' and 'Yea' – or have lost special social or psychological connotations – as have 'freely' and 'desire' – but many words and much of the syntax are simple and straightforward. Even a complicated state of mind is expressed in everyday terms:

It were as possible for me to say I lov'd nothing so well as you; but believe me not, and yet I lie not; I confess nothing, nor I deny nothing. I am sorry for my cousin.

(ll. 269–71)

When Benedick's reply cuts through these contradictory statements its boldness and danger would be immediately apparent if swords were still worn and used. So would the wildness and mockery of her response, in which 'it' stands for the words of the oath, with a laughable glance at the sword that he may now be grasping;

> – By my sword, Beatrice, thou lovest me.
> – Do not swear, and eat it.

Action, what is spoken, and sensation are all extreme and unusual. Rapid thought, deep passion, personal and present danger, disbelief, and, possibly, laughter will all have their place in performance and yet verbal expression is no more than any person might use.

Sometimes it is a fleeting perception that has an everyday currency and holds down a strange circumstance or subtle thought, so that what happens is not entirely unfamiliar. The opening lines of *Henry the Fourth, Part One* are an example:

KING   So shaken as we are, so wan with care,
       Find we a time for frighted peace to pant
       And breathe short-winded accents of new broils
       To be commenc'd in strands afar remote.

At the start of this play an audience may not comprehend the political situation or the threat of 'broils' but the words *pant* and *short-winded* are immediately accessible and, when accompanied by a performance that is physically 'shaken' and 'wan with care', they ensure that a very basic weakness and uncertainty will not fail to register. Much is fantastic and strange in *Cymbeline*, a romantic narrative play that came late in Shakespeare's career, encompasses warfare and off-stage death, and was printed along with the tragedies in the First Folio edition of Shakespeare's plays, and yet its text repeatedly invites an audience's response to immediately recognizable events and simple physical actions. Imogen says she would have watched her departing husband:

... till he had melted from
The smallness of a gnat to air, and then
Have turn'd mine eye and wept.

(I.iii.20–2)

When the Soothsayer brings all the stories to their conclusion, his words draw attention to fingers that tune an
instrument, so that the gods seem to participate in this familiar business while directing the fate of mankind: 'The
fingers of the pow'rs above do tune / The harmony of
this peace' (V.v.464–5).

Simple actions can work to the same effect as simple
words. Another late play, *Coriolanus*, introduces small
physical details, which are described in stage directions
or implicit in the dialogue and are immediately recognizable; for example:

> *Enter* VOLUMNIA *and* VIRGILIA, *mother and wife to Marcius;*
> *they set them down on two low stools and sew.*

(I.iii.0, SD)

and

> *A long flourish. They all cry* 'Marcius, Marcius!' *cast up*
> *their caps and lances. Cominius and Lartius stand bare.*

(I.ix.40, SD)

The best known and most crucial of the stage directions
specifying ordinary actions comes when Coriolanus listens
to his mother and decides to withdraw the Volscian army
from the gates of Rome: '*He holds her by the hand, silent*'
(V.iii.182, SD). Before this he had risen from his seat and
'turned away' while saying nothing; the women and his
son have been kneeling before him. Now simple words
follow the holding of hands, 'O mother, mother! / What
have you done?' Repeatedly in this play, actions register
strongly in silence, not least those of his wife Virgilia,
whom he calls 'My gracious silence' (II.i.166).

Sometimes Shakespeare's dialogue carries an instruction that involves a more comprehensive and wordless

response; for example, from *Othello*: 'Alas, why gnaw you so your nether lip?' (V.ii.46). At other times in this play the requirement is very precise, as in 'Let me see your eyes; look in my face', or occasionally, too minute for an actor to follow adequately, as in 'Mine eyes do itch; / Doth that bode weeping?' (IV.ii. 25 and IV.iii.56–7). Othello's final speech describes how his

> ... subdu'd eyes,
> Albeit unused to the melting mood,
> Drops tears as fast as the Arabian trees
> Their med'cinable gum.

> (V.ii.351–4)

A reader's imagination, if fully engaged, is likely to supply the tears more suitably than an actor can make them actually present and an audience-member may become closely involved with the action of the play as imagination 'amends' the actor's performance (see Chapter 7, p. 176).

When words fail or are hard to understand, the introduction of an everyday action or simple turn of phrase has a double effect, both encouraging the audience's recognition of what is happening and offering the actor an opportunity to improvise so that words and action can be freshly and intimately enacted. When Hamlet has just seen the Ghost of his father and accepted his duty to set right the time in which he lives he joins his friends with the very ordinary 'Come, let's go together.' Later, having killed Polonius, he greets the sound of soldiers coming to find him with 'O, here they come.' In the final scene he breaks off talk about death and providence with the simple 'Let be', a homely phrase found only in the Second Quarto, the early edition thought to be printed from an autograph copy. Later, the same phrase slightly varied – 'But let it be' – is in the Folio text as well as the Quarto's, after a speech in which Hamlet has carefully considered his own death.[2]

A thorough study of a text will try to assess the effect of all moments that bring the play into close focus with words that are immediately comprehensible and actions that are familiar and can actually happen on stage. How significant these incidents are is a matter for individual judgement, taking into account where they come in the narrative, who is involved and how performance is affected, and how they relate to what has previously been said and done. Repetitions occurring later will also be significant: for example, the *nothings* of Cordelia and Lear are echoed and redefined in the same opening scene and yet again by Gloucester and his son Edmund in the next scene, by Lear speaking with the fool in his next scene, and by Edgar when in disguise as Poor Tom in Act III, scene iv. With repetition, the wordless moments in *Coriolanus* and the tears in *Othello* develop greater significance and have a different effect on an audience.

The many changes that time has brought to how we live and think tend to make us less impressed by a sense of the actual in performance than were Shakespeare's first audiences. Actuality as shown on film and television and in countless photographs has become too familiar to make the same impression on us. In Shakespeare's day there were no intimate biographies or autobiographies to read, and no novels that offered a detailed and personal view of day-to-day existence. English painting at the time was nearly always iconic and to our eyes often seems inexpert and wooden. Lifelike impressions were likely to be found only in privately owned miniatures or etchings imported from mainland Europe. Book illustrations, monumental sculpture, or ecclesiastical stained glass offered few details that can now seem to be taken from life. In contrast to us, Shakespeare's audiences crowded to newly built theatres to see famous heroes and people like themselves presented on stage and acted 'to the life'.[3] This means that when studying Shakespeare's plays we should be prepared to allow even a passing tremor of actual behaviour or brief echo of everyday speech to have a greater effect than we would ordinarily assume.

* * *

On some occasions, that are more frequent in the later plays, everyday words and activities have a prolonged effect so that an entire encounter can seem to take place within the spectators' own living-space and to be comprehensible in almost the same terms as their own lives, although to more powerful effect. Two scenes in *King Lear* are prime examples. In both, the king is physically very weak, which at once marks him out from everyone else by requiring the actor to modify his manner of speech and physical energy. As he lies before Cordelia with his medical needs attended to and music playing, Lear's words could scarcely be more simple although charged far beyond their usual weight of feeling and meaning:

> You do me wrong to take me out o' th' grave.
> Thou art a soul in bliss; but I am bound
> Upon a wheel of fire, that mine own tears
> Do scald like molten lead.
>
> (IV.vii.45–8)

Gradually everyday concerns are introduced and accompanied by simple actions so that before the short scene ends, what Lear says and does will be immediately recognizable: 'Where have I been? Where am I? ... I know not what to say. / I will not swear these are my hands. Let's see. / I feel this pin prick.' When Cordelia asks him to 'look upon' her, he has to be restrained: 'No, sir, you must not kneel' (l. 59). Assured that she is indeed his daughter, he touches her face, saying: 'Be your tears wet? Yes, faith. I pray weep not' (l. 71). Contact between them has been established slowly and intimately, and with a gentle touch. Now Lear's speech will be quiet and, with no one interrupting, take its own slow pace so that an audience, perhaps straining to hear, is drawn to share in his accumulated pain and awakening happiness. He leaves the stage, not as a king but as a frail old man who knows that he needs the understanding and support of others: 'You must bear with me. / Pray you now, forget and forgive; I am old and foolish' (ll. 84–5).

Lear's last scene starts with a tremendous burst of anger and a poignant sense of betrayal but then moves less certainly so that those watching believe 'He knows not what he says; and vain it is / That we present us to him' (V.iii.293–4). While the actor must have some understanding of what Lear is saying, sentence-by-sentence and word-by-word, members of an audience will tend to give their own meanings to what he says as they watch closely or try to avert their eyes. When Lear realizes that Cordelia is gone for ever and that his own death is near, 'Pray you undo this button' (l. 309) marks how he is struggling to breathe as any invalid would do when suffering a stroke. The following 'Thank you, sir' is possibly more remarkable since it shows a consideration for someone unknown or unrecognized that has no precedent in all that this king has said before, the everyday phrase marking a new dependence and humility. The Quarto text follows this with an inarticulate and sustained cry, represented as 'O, o, o, o', but in the Folio, Lear dies asking others to see what he sees, and repeats this several times as if there were no more to say or want: 'Do you see this? Look on her. Look, her lips. / Look there, look there!' Although Kent tries to make contact with him, dropping the disguise in which he has supported his master, for most of Lear's last moments on stage those present with him draw little attention to themselves but act as a chorus to give a lead to the audience's responses. As an earlier chapter has shown (see page 60, above), the narrative of this awesome tragedy draws to its close with the death of a king presented by means of simple words and actions that anyone can understand and to which the actor has to give particular life and meaning suitable to each performance. It should also be noted that the physical performance that an audience witnesses will echo what anyone has experienced who has watched helplessly as a dear friend or close relative slowly dies.

The last moments of Cleopatra could scarcely be more different. She commands the stage, dressed for a regal occasion and speaking with sustained and elaborate brilliance. After she has poisoned herself and sits stone-still in state, she continues to draw all eyes on stage and in the audience; as Octavius Caesar will say:

> ... she looks like sleep,
> As she would catch another Antony
> In her strong toil of grace.
>   (*Antony and Cleopatra*, V.ii.343–5)

She possesses 'grace' – blessed, beautiful, influential – and has a mysterious and dangerous strength since *toil* can signify strife, strenuous labour, or turmoil, as well as a net, snare, or trap. Nevertheless, amongst all this grandeur, everyday activities accompany her approach to death. Putting venomous asps to her breast mirrors a domestic gesture, identified in Cleopatra's 'Dost thou not see my baby at my breast / That sucks the nurse asleep?' (ll. 307–8) – an image that marks a new awareness since, only moments before, she had proclaimed 'I have nothing / Of woman in me' (ll. 237–8). The actual moment of death comes unexpectedly so that she leaves a sentence unfinished and the crown she wears lurches to one side, so much 'awry' that Charmian will have to 'mend' the regal image (ll. 316–17). This 'high event' (l. 357) has been given an injection of everyday reality that counter-states its marvels and brings the acting of the play a little closer to the audience's own sense-experiences.

This tragedy has two fabulous and commanding protagonists, both speaking with glowing eloquence, and yet, half way through in their one quiet and sustained scene together, they are tongue-tied and elements of ordinary behaviour are conspicuously and continuously present, at times being the only means of expression. Antony's forces have been defeated so shamefully at sea that he believes 'the land bids me tread no more upon't ... I / Have lost my way for ever' (III.xi.1–4). When Cleopatra had become alarmed and ordered her ship away from battle, he had left 'the fight in height' (III.x.21) and is now so ashamed that he tells his soldiers to leave him, take his treasure, and fend for themselves. When they refuse, he repeats the order in simple but pressured and broken phrases:

> Leave me, I pray, a little; pray you now;
> Nay, do so, for indeed I have lost command,
> Therefore I pray you. I'll see you by and by.
>
> (III.iii.22–4)

The soldiers say nothing and, although modern editors usually mark a simple *Exeunt* here, the original text of the Folio has no stage direction; some men may be slow to leave, now that military order is lost. A stage direction '*Sits down.*' holds the focus on Antony and its abruptness might imply that, without ceremony, he sinks down to the stage floor where he has been standing. At this very moment Cleopatra enters, attended as Antony had been but saying nothing, even when begged to do so. She is probably supported physically because she later asks to be allowed to sit. This action mirrors Antony's entry but the two lovers make no contact at first:

> EROS   Nay, gentle madam, to him. Comfort him.
> IRAS   Do, most dear Queen.
> CHARMIAN   Do? Why, what else?
> CLEOPATRA   Let me sit down. O Juno!
> ANTONY   No, no, no, no, no.
> EROS   See you here, sir?
> ANTONY   O, fie, fie, fie!
> CHARMIAN   Madam!
> IRAS   Madam, O good Empress!
> EROS   Sir, sir!
>
> (ll. 25–34)

All these words are simple and ordinary but the impasse at the centre of attention is not, both persons being unable to acknowledge each other's presence. Antony's monosyllabic repetitions show that his mind is somewhere else, and as he later makes clear, occupied in memories of Octavius: 'Yes, my lord, yes. He at Philippi kept / His sword e'en like a dancer ...'. An audience will know

far more about what holds the two principals apart than
anyone says at this time.

Eventually contact is made. A dismissive 'no matter'
finishes Antony's reverie and then Cleopatra slowly takes
the initiative, asking her attendants for support. Eros
goes to prepare Antony:

> Most noble sir, arise; the Queen approaches.
> Her head's declin'd, and death will seize her but
> > [i.e. *unless*]
> Your comfort makes the rescue.
>
> > (ll. 46–8)

Incomplete verse-lines indicate numerous pauses before
Antony speaks directly to her: 'O, whither has thou led
me, Egypt? See / How I convey my shame ...'. Her reply
completes his verse-line with two simple exclamations,
the first acknowledging her dependence, the second
begging his forgiveness:

> > > O my lord, my lord,
> > Forgive my fearful sails! I little thought
> > You would have followed.
> ANTONY > > > Egypt, thou knew'st too well
> > My heart was to thy rudder tied by th' strings,
> > And thou shouldst tow me after... .
>
> > (ll. 54–8)

As he continues, she twice begs pardon and is now so responsive to what he says that, when the lead in the duologue is exchanged in mid-line, the iambics continue to
go forward. At this point physical performance takes over
from speech, at first when she weeps and then when they
come close together for a kiss, no longer needing to say
anything:

> CLEOPATRA > > > Pardon, pardon!
> ANTONY > Fall not a tear, I say; one of them rates
> > All that is won and lost. Give me a kiss.
>
> > (ll. 68–70)

The meeting has gone forward so slowly and uncertainly that a spectator will have been encouraged to follow intently and now, in the silence of the kiss, both protagonists will be seen as if in close-up. More short phrases and disturbed lines of verse follow, before the scene concludes with a burst of energy expressed in a rhymed couplet:

> Even this repays me.
> We sent our schoolmaster; is 'a come back?
> Love, I am full of lead. Some wine,
> Within there, and our viands! Fortune knows
> We scorn her most when most she offers blows.
>   *Exeunt.*

In its own way, this short, unequally shared, inwardly disturbed, and simply worded duologue makes as strong an effect as the sustained rhetoric and poetry or the clash of armies in other scenes. Careful phrasing and halting rhythm encourage an audience to respond as if this reconciliation is actually happening. The persons of the fabled story are far from ordinary but, by remembering what has happened earlier in the play and by drawing on their own memories and imaginations, members of an audience may believe that they have shared in a real-life experience. In Shakespeare's day, such lifelikeness in a theatrical tragedy would have been surprising, and possibly shocking.

In later plays Shakespeare explored many different ways of bringing the drama close to the audience's own experience. In the last scene of *The Winter's Tale*, the statue of Hermione is displayed at first as an entirely artificial object but as it comes to life, with all eyes on stage fixed upon it and to the sound of music, the theatre audience will also watch closely to catch a sight of its very first movements and so become increasingly aware of Hermione coming to life in the actor's true-life presence. When Leontes extends his hand to her on Paulina's instructions, his exclamation and two very simple words respond to a sensuous reality and then, in a silence highlighted by the chorus of Polixenes and Camillo, the physical actions of king and queen become as ordinary as those of any two persons held speechless in each other's bodily presence:

> LEONTES   O, she's warm!
>   If this be magic, let it be an art
>   Lawful as eating.
> POLIXENES   She embraces him.
> CAMILLO   She hangs about his neck.
>   If she pertain to life, let her speak too.
>   (V.iii.109–13)

Shakespeare used a more extended sequence of silent activity in the very last moments of *The Tempest*. When Prospero invites everyone on stage to enter his 'cell', the private place where, for twelve years, he has lived alone with his daughter and has kept the books that held the secrets of his 'so mighty art', his words could scarcely be more simple or modestly polite: 'Please you, draw near.' This is followed by a mutual silence and protracted movements across the entire stage as everyone, in due order, passes by Prospero and over the threshold. Each one will walk in a distinctive way and exchange very different looks with their host: the king who is now accepted into Prospero's family, the son and daughter betrothed to marry, the old and trusted counsellor, the two would-be murderers, one of whom, moments before, 'to call brother / Would even infect [Prospero's] mouth' (ll. 131). At this very last moment, the simple '*Exeunt omnes*' of the Folio text offers the actors absolute freedom to play their parts according to each individual's sense of the confrontation. Each one will act differently as they are led by their performances earlier in the play and in response to the audience's reception of all that they have done. This departure from the stage and the play will be a lengthy process and what an audience makes of it all will vary with each of its members and on each occasion. Then, the actor who has been Prospero steps forward as the man he is in life, to speak to the audience.

Time and again in Shakespeare's plays, actors are required to give an impression of actual lived experience or,
in other words, to re-create life itself on stage. Today this
might be called theatrical realism, but not the scenic
realism that re-creates an actual environment on stage: any
scenery that is provided and even the stage itself will tend
to disappear when the actors closely 'shadow' the lives of
their audiences.[4] The realism of Shakespeare's plays may
be called performative because it gives a sense of actual
life by being embodied in the physical presence of the
actors. Intermittently it exists alongside the most amazing
events. Kings, queens, servants, beggars, supernatural
beings, and children exist alongside each other in this
created world, men and women who suffer pain and those
who are full of joy and peace, and others who are mad,
cunning, destructive, irresistibly funny, or eloquent and
resourceful beyond all expectation. The extraordinary
nature of Shakespeare's plays will be obvious to everyone
who sees or reads them, but their actuality will remain a
quality best discovered when experiencing them in performance or taking special care in reading. When studying
the texts, enough time should be allowed to imagine their
lifelikeness and its varied and variable implications.

* * *

While sustained presentation of everyday behaviour is
mostly found in Shakespeare's later plays, all of them are
at least touched by actuality. This is especially true of the
comedies that take place within households and that deal
with more familiar matters than histories or tragedies.
The dialogue of *Twelfth Night*, for example, requires ordinary actions to be carried out: 'For saying so, there's
gold' – 'Let me see thee caper. Ha, higher! Ha, ha, excellent!' – 'Give me my veil; come, throw it o'er my face' –
'Let me see your face' – 'She returns this ring… . If it be
worth stooping for, there it lies in your eye' – 'I extend
my hand to him, thus, quenching my familiar smile' –
'Hold, there's expenses for thee' – 'Let the garden door

be shut, and leave me to my hearing. Give me your hand, sir.'[5] In early performances all this physical activity would have been immediately recognizable as if in ordinary life, and much of it will have the same effect today. Modes of behaviour and instinctive physical reactions are also pre-scribed: 'like a cloistress, she will veiled walk' – 'She made good view of me' – 'I will be proud, I will read politic authors, I will baffle Sir Toby... . I am happy. I will be strange, stout, in yellow stockings, and cross-garter'd, even with the swiftness of putting on.'[6]

Similar directives in the comedy's last scene call for everyday behaviour that is both varied and distinctive. The normal manners of a class-conscious society are modified and put to strange use in the first exchange:

> FABIAN Now, as thou lov'st me, let me see his letter.
> CLOWN Good Master Fabian, grant me another request.
> FABIAN Anything.
> CLOWN Do not desire to see this letter.
> FABIAN This is to give a dog, and in recompense
> desire my dog again.
>
> (V.i.1–6)

Several small details would have signified a great deal in early performances. Between Feste, the clown, and Fabian, the servant, 'lov'st' and 'Good Master ... grant my request' invite ironically genteel behaviour until talk of giving 'a dog' brings that to an abrupt and rougher end.[7] Contrastingly open and gracious behaviour is seen the next moment, when the noble Count Orsino enters and ad-dresses these two as 'friends', asking Feste, 'How dost thou, my good fellow?' Class difference and deportment are then normalized when he gives gold to Feste, who in return re-peatedly asks for more; Orsino responds to the clown's fooling by addressing him as 'you', not with the more famil-iar 'thou', as at first. Many details in the dialogue call for physical actions that would have been immediately recog-nizable and meaningful to the play's first audiences: Antonio brought on stage under arrest; Viola, as Cesario, accused as a 'most ingrateful boy'; Olivia entering silently when asked to do so and then speaking briefly but boldly to Orsino and turning to address Cesario before he can reply. When Orsino interrupts with 'Gracious Olivia' and she ignores him they both ignore familiar protocol. The entries of a priest to give evidence, Sir Andrew and Sir Toby on their way to find a surgeon, and Sebastian, to apologize and ask for pardon, were cues for a variety of stage business that reflects and modifies ordinary living. Here and elsewhere, the presence on stage of everyday activity brought the fantasy of this comedy home to the roots it shares with the everyday life of its first audiences and emphasizes the transgressions of that norm. How far this happens in performances today will depend on the ability of director, designers, and actors to find meaningful alternatives. In the imagination of readers, some of the original freshness of invention may be recaptured by studying how Shakespeare's contemporaries lived and thought.

In *Macbeth*, social protocol is established and violated repeatedly. The banquet scene in Act III, scene iv, is introduced with incomplete verse-lines that indicate silences while routine activities are taking place; allowing time for this will help today's audiences to understand what is happening:

> MACBETH   You know your own degrees, sit down.
>   At first and last the hearty welcome.
> LORDS   Thanks to your Majesty.
> MACBETH   Our self will mingle with society
>   And play the humble host.
>   Our hostess keeps her state; but in best time
>   We will require her welcome.
>
>   (III.iv.1–6)

With the two appearances of Banquo's ghost every action is skewed out of the ordinary, culminating with the assembled company's response to Lady Macbeth's:

>   At once, good night.
>   Stand not upon the order of your going,
>   But go at once.
>
>   (ll. 118–20)

Thanes and servants have to find their way off stage
without any scripted words and their behaviour will
become closer to ordinary life as the actors draw variously on their own experiences of embarrassment, suspicion, mutiny, or relief on escaping from danger. As the
new king and queen sit down alone amongst the wreck-
age of the banquet, some touches of ordinary and familiar behaviour may briefly register in the consciousness
of an audience and emphasize the ominous transformation from public ceremony. Macbeth's next words take
the drama forward to nightmare terrors by sensuous
evocation and prediction. Then he speaks with a new
resolve to enter that awesome world, where nothing will
be familiar.

* * *

Most members of a Globe audience would have had little
or no chance in real life of viewing such royal and noble
persons as those at the centre of the tragedies, but class
distinctions and formal ceremonies worked in similar
ways at all levels of society. What happened on stage was
made more immediately recognizable and personally relevant by the inclusion of persons who would be familiar
to audiences. The cast of *Macbeth* includes a porter for
the castle-gate, a nameless but revered old man, a group
of children with their mother, a doctor with a nurse, a
nameless messenger, and the young son of a famous
soldier. The much earlier *Romeo and Juliet*, about two
noble families, starts mundanely with the boorish talk,
bad jokes, insults and brawling of rival serving-men –
'heartless hinds', the well-connected Tybalt calls them
(I.i.64) – and the Nurse in Capulet's household is an old
and favoured servant, quite at ease with everyone. In
preparation for Juliet's wedding, the head of the household busies himself by making a very ordinary fuss with
his servants about inviting guests, hiring extra cooks,
ordering 'baked meats' for guests and logs for firing the
ovens, and generally 'play[ing] the huswife for this once'

(IV.ii.1–10 and 43; IV.iv.3–21). Musicians who were hired for the wedding are given time to talk about their wages, skills, rivalries, and the next meal. At the start of the last Act of *Hamlet,* the two clowns who enter to dig graves are given the stage to talk among themselves until one is sent off to fetch a 'stoup of liquor' and the other starts singing while he digs up skulls and bones.

The early history plays have small roles for persons engaged in work that would be familiar to most members of the Globe audiences. Thomas Horner the armourer with Peter his man, Dick the butcher, and Smith the weaver are needed for *Henry the Sixth, Part Two.* Two Keepers, three Watchmen, and a Huntsman, all nameless, are briefly involved with the principal persons of *Henry the Sixth, Part Three,* and, in roles more symbolic than necessary for the narrative, 'a Son that has killed his father' and 'a Father that has killed his son'. In the two Parts of the later *Henry the Fourth,* scenes take place in the Boar's Head tavern of Eastcheap, at a posthouse on the road into London, and in the grounds of a Gloucestershire manor house. The persons encountered in these places have very ordinary jobs to do: Gadshill among both carriers and a chamberlain; Mistress Quickly and the drawers who serve customers at the tavern, and Doll Tearsheet the local whore. Prince Hal in these plays, before he becomes King Henry the Fifth, spends time with Poins, Bardolph, Peto and Mistress Quickly, all of whom might bear some resemblance to unprivileged members of early audiences. As the history plays followed one after another, Shakespeare added more and more roles that would take the action into the actual world of his own time so that past events might seem to be happening in the present. This development is seen at its fullest in *Henry V,* of 1599, which has whole scenes in both England and France peopled with ordinary soldiers with ordinary names, and a group of captains who in timeless ways represent England, Scotland, Ireland, and Wales. During the siege of Harfleur a nameless boy gives his own view of the soldiers he is serving, and, before peace is concluded, Lieutenant Pistol has a soliloquy in which he foresees his post-war future as a bawd and cutpurse back home in London.

Much that was ordinary to Shakespeare and his first audiences is now exceptional and no longer current. Research is needed to uncover the full extent of this seam that runs through all the plays and care has to be taken before it can be re-presented with comparable life-likeness in present-day performances. An amazingly detailed and once familiar world is hidden within the texts and some new nugget of it is likely to be unearthed wherever one starts to investigate. We no longer wear swords in the city or metal armour on a battlefield, nor do we travel by horse on unpaved roads, nor is it difficult to communicate with each other or keep up with national and local news. A large proportion of the country is no longer covered with woodland or forest, our homes have heating and light. Personal relationships in families and everyday behaviour are not those of a class-ordered and settled society. Fundamental changes have occurred in the institution of marriage, sexual mores and practices, aims and availability of education, religious belief and practices, the prevalent philosophies and scientific understanding. Weekly attendance at church ceased to be legally enforced centuries ago; theft and sedition are no longer capital offences. All these circumstances and others that made the lives of Shakespeare's contemporaries different from our own are found throughout the plays and must have affected the response of their first audiences by echoing their own thoughts and experiences.

Innumerable changes have obscured how close the men and women of the plays were to the lives of their audiences. For us what happens on stage will always be to some degree strange and remarkable, just as the language will be, and in both this will be increasingly so as time goes on. There are two major consequences. First, the texts have become a favoured and profitable ground for historical study because they provide examples of social and intellectual life that are more readily comprehensible than the legal documents or descriptive writings of the time. The other principal effect occurs in performance. As Shakespeare's dialogue comes alive in the present through physical and affective performance, so the on-stage actions are received by the senses and what is out-of-date behaviour is seen to partake of the present-day reality of the actors themselves. Because Shakespeare wrote dialogue imagining the speakers to be alive in every way – in what they do, as well as what they say – performance of the plays can raise echoes in the memories of today's audiences and, out of date though much will be, reflect their day-to-day experiences, and arouse their imaginations to give an element of contemporary lifelikeness to all that happens on stage. This would be astonishing had we not become accustomed to experiencing this apparently indestructible quality in Shakespeare's plays.

* * *

The everyday activities that made these plays lifelike for their original audiences, however fantastic, ideal, or simplified their action might be, were also those elements that were closest to Shakespeare's own personal experiences. That does not imply that any persons in their casts are portraits of himself or individuals known to him, or that the texts hold clues to specific events in his life. The life-likeness of the plays derives from the self-evident fact that nothing can come from the mind of any writer that has not first entered there through the senses during day-to-day living or, in second-hand and less palpable form, through reading and listening to the reports of other lives and events. Shakespeare must have had an insatiable appetite for taking notice of people and physical phenomena as well as the imagination and skill to write as if he were, in his own mind, the very varied persons speaking the dialogue of the plays and directly involved in their action.

Fostering this ability was an essential part of a poet's task as described by Horace in his *Art of Poetry*, a treatise echoed by many Renaissance writers and rendered into English verse by Ben Jonson. 'It is not enough for poems to be fine,' wrote Horace, 'they must charm, and draw the mind of the listener at will.' He explained the implications of this for drama in the advice he gave to tragic actors:

> As the human face answers a smile with a smile, so does it wait upon tears; if you would have me weep, you must first of all feel grief yourself; then and not till then will your misfortunes, Telephus or Peleus, touch me. If the part assigned you is not in character, I shall fall asleep or laugh.[8]

In line with this advice, Shakespeare wrote parts that could be played as if the fictional people were actually alive. In imagination he had entered into their beings – bodies and minds – so that he could experience and give expression to the sensations of each moment they were on stage. A similar transference of consciousness and sensation is common between two individuals who care for each other deeply and know each other intimately; it is far more rare among playwrights, especially over the wide range of persons who inhabit Shakespeare's plays.

Religion offered another tradition of 'possessing' the very being of other persons. Devout Christians addressed the saints and Christ himself as if they were actually present, and begged them to 'enter' into their lives and minds so that they might be informed by their spirits. The Elizabethan prayer book, heard each week during required church attendance, called on the congregation, after it had joined in the 'general confession', to 'hear what Christ sayeth to all that truly turn to him', the present tense being used as if He were actually present. The congregation was exhorted to follow in His footsteps and, in the act of communion, to be present at Christ's 'table' where the Last Supper was re-enacted 'in remembrance of His death and passion'. When writing *The*

Epistle to the Galatians, Saint Paul imagined that he was participating in the crucifixion:

> For I through the Law am dead to the Law and, that I might live unto God, *I am crucified with Christ.* Thus I live, yet not I now, but Christ liveth in me.[9]

We cannot know to what extent Shakespeare was attentive at church services but many hundreds of passages in the plays are proof that the words of the Bible and Book of Common Prayer had entered deeply into his consciousness. Without being aware of it, participation in those acts of worship and devotion that assumed direct contact with the saints, and with Christ himself, might have encouraged a similar intimate and active relationship with the persons of the plays.[10]

The effect of this 'in-dwelling' – to use this religious term in a secular sense – is most evident where most constant and mysterious, that is in the phrasing, timing, shape, and weight of the dialogue. When spoken imaginatively and with skill, Shakespeare's words can seem to be impelled by sensation as well as thought, as if speech has taken its natural form at the moment of engagement in the ongoing action. Shakespeare's facility in this respect is found everywhere in the plays, however refined, heightened, or simple the writing. Almost all the quotations of dialogue in this book exemplify something of this lifelikeness. Computers enable us to analyse and compare the writing for different moments or speakers but they are unable to deal with all the relevant evidence because they do not breathe to make the necessary sounds and have no bodies to be engaged in speech and action. The lifelikeness inherent everywhere in Shakespeare's dialogue can best be experienced and studied in rehearsal and performance, where the pleasure and confidence that present-day actors find in speaking the words and embodying the persons of the plays show that much of the quality of actual speech has survived the passage of time despite all the changes of language, social custom, human behaviour, and culture.

Even unskilled readers can discover this lifelikeness for themselves by a committed speaking aloud of a number of lines and by imagining themselves to be the speaker. After trying several different ways of saying the words, including some that are unlikely to be right, they can choose the most coherently meaningful and speak the lines again without hesitation. Then they will begin to discover how the words are able to carry the impress of actual thought and natural instincts.

Even a few lines with complicated verse-structure or obscure in meaning can seem to possess both heightened expression and the accent of authentic speech. In this respect, the everyday is almost everywhere present in the plays, and, in Horace's words, can 'draw the minds' of an audience so that the fiction is believed and its sensations shared. This sense of the actual is not easily appreciated on the page, but in performance it enfranchises poetry as the language of persons whose thoughts and feelings are like our own.

* * *

The extraordinary nature of Shakespeare's plays is evident on a first reading. Words, syntax, versification, story, action, the persons of the play, the intensity or elevation of some passages and the obscurity of others, all mark this writing apart from what is familiar and natural in our lives. To offset this very just first impression and gain a firmer hold on the text, one of the first tasks of study might be to look for the text's other face, whose features are ordinary and immediately accessible for any audience. Speeches that offer no linguistic difficulties and could readily be translated into another language provide a useful point of departure for studying the everyday actuality of the dialogue and sensing its consequences for actors and audiences. While only performance by skilled and experienced actors can reveal the full extent of this lifelikeness in the words, a reader who speaks the dialogue aloud will begin to hear the accents of ordinary speech within its sensitive and compelling music. Taking note of stage directions and textual references that call for activities that could happen any day and in any place will similarly help a reader to visualize what is happening on stage. Slowly a student can draw closer to the plays. They will never be less than extraordinary but Shakespeare's imagination has brought all their marvels to immediate and believable life, and study, like acting, can help to sense that achievement by relating the texts to life-experiences of the present day, and to what can be learnt about those of Shakespeare's time.

Notes

1. *As You Like It*, IV.i.193–4; *Much Ado*, V.iv.97; *Twelfth Night*, I.v.238; *Richard III*, V.iii.182–3; *Henry IV, Part 2*, IV.v.92; *Othello*, V.ii.284.
2. *Hamlet*, I.v.190, IV.ii.2–3 and V.ii.217, 330.
3. The phrase is taken from *Coriolanus*, III.ii.106.
4. See *A Midsummer Night's Dream*, V.i.209–11.
5. I.ii.18; I.iii.132–3; I.v.156, 215; II.ii.4 and 12–13; II.v.61–2; III.i.41–2 and 89–90.
6. I.i.28; II.ii.17; II.v.143–57.
7. Proverbially, dogs could be fierce and quarrelsome. The Oxford editors (Oxford University Press, 1994), Roger Warren and Stanley Wells, suggest an allusion to Dr Bullein's response to the Queen when she asked for the gift of his dog and promised to give him whatever he desired in recompense. This might have been current gossip in the MiddleTemple, where the comedy had an early performance, because it is recorded only in the *Diary* of the templar, Sir John Massingham.
8. Horace, *Ars Poetica*, §99, tr. E. H. Blakeney (London: Scholartis Press, 1928), p. 45.
9. Galatians, 2. 19–20; Bishops' Bible, 1586, italics added.
10. Renaissance painters commonly placed portraits of patrons or self-portraits in depictions of biblical events.

7

Seeing Double: Uncertainty and Choice

Anyone who has worked on a theatre production will have a keen understanding of failure. As an actor, you can be left with 'egg on your face', stripped of all pretence, alone and exposed to the audience, perhaps laughed at, mocked, or sent off the stage. An author may have to listen when words fail to hold attention or make no sense at all, while an actor struggles to 'make them work'. A stage-manager or, as Elizabethans would say, a bookkeeper will sometimes be unable to prevent the wrong person entering or a technical device failing to function. Sometimes an entire company of actors must face an audience that has lost interest or become hostile. Behind any success in theatre lies the possibility of failure, when the only recourse is to recognize what has happened, try to ride the unmanageable beast, and learn from the experience.

Shakespeare as actor, author, and part-owner of a company would have had first-hand experience of what failure means and this has left its mark on the plays. We have seen that, at some significant moments, words or action prove insufficient and the play continues in silence until words again express a new understanding or objective.[1] At other times the text requires performance to become ridiculous, and dramatic illusion to break down, before the play can continue. By using various kinds of failure Shakespeare was able to present a double view of a

167

play, alternative illusions that leave an audience free to
choose which it prefers or try to enjoy them both.

* * *

Actors in the early *Love's Labour's Lost* (1588–94) are
asked to accept, or to fake, the embarrassment of total
failure. '*The Pageant of the Worthies*' stands little chance of
success when it is performed as a concluding celebration,
its dialogue being so obviously absurd and the five actors
so ill-suited to their roles as super-heroes of ancient myth.
Today the entertainment would be called a parody
because it imitates the erudite shows of welcome, compliment, and propaganda that were common at the time,
and ridicules these 'triumphs' by exaggerating their style
of presentation. But more than this is happening on
stage: Shakespeare was not confined by a critical category
that was rarely or never used by his contemporaries and
each new entry to the pageant does more than make
parodic fun of literary and theatrical artifice. They all
lead to a moment when the actor faces failure.

Shakespeare might not have known what a parody was
because the word was not current in English printed
texts. Its first entry in the *Oxford Dictionary* is from Ben
Jonson's *Every Man in His Humour* and dated 1598. In
fact the word occurs only in Jonson's revised version of
this comedy, published in 1616 and first performed no
earlier than 1605. Even then the word is used in a literary and pedantic context and introduced as the very
latest in learned discourse, which has to be explained
before it is understood. In the first version of the
comedy set in Italy, Matheo, is condemned for stealing
the first lines of Daniel's *Delia* and passing them off as
his own. In the revised play, re-located in London,
Matthew, the town gull, has altered the poem and, when
Justice Clement declares it to be stolen, young Master
Knowell calls out, 'A parody! A parody!' and then explains that its author had 'a kind of miraculous gift to
make it absurder than it was'.[2] Shakespeare may have

acted in this play since he is named as an actor in the 1616 edition of Jonson's *Works* but he never used the word *parody* in his own plays and not until the end of the seventeenth century did it begin to be common in English literary usage; in less specialized writing its arrival was some time later. While parody as a genre was recognized by Greek and Latin critics from Aristotle onwards and is relevant to parts of well-known classical texts, such as Ovid's *Metamorphoses* (available in Arthur Golding's translation of 1565), it was not well represented in English in Shakespeare's day, his plays being published long before translations of Aristophanes or Petronius, the great masters of parody.

As we read '*The Pageant of the Worthies*', its parodic humour may seem uppermost but, in performance, we find that imitation and ridicule were not Shakespeare's principal concerns and that other responses have greater effect. Following each actor's entry, theatrical failure strikes and grand illusions collapse. The onstage audience does not sit back and enjoy the parody; its members interrupt the performance and, in effect, make an alternative show by exhibiting their own cleverness with the result that, one after another, each actor in the pageant stops acting, no longer able to speak the words he has studied. Sir Nathaniel, the local curate, is at first 'dismay'd' by this response to his efforts and soon quite 'overthrown' so that he has to be taken away by Costard, the clown (V.ii.558–79). Holofernes, the schoolmaster, twice confesses that he is 'put out of countenance' by his audience and, being unable to recover confidence, he takes himself off with a reproach: 'This is not generous, not gentle, not humble' (ll. 600, 613 and 621). As Hector, the Spanish knight Don Adriano de Armado has sufficient self-control to stop his performance twice and ask for attention before he proceeds (ll. 642, 647–8 and 654–5). Only Moth is able to act without interruption, except from the schoolmaster who warns him, probably in a loud stage whisper, 'Keep some state in thy exit, and vanish' (V.ii.587). Holofernes had introduced the boy in inflated, unnecessarily varied, and, as we would say, parodic hyperbole:

> Great Hercules is presented by this imp,
> Whose club kill'd Cerberus, that three-headed *canus*;
> And when he was a babe, a child, a shrimp,
> Thus did he strangle serpents in his *manus*.
> *Quoniam* he seemeth in minority,
> *Ergo* I come with this apology.

(V.ii.581–6)

On these cues, Moth, who has been given no words to say, will probably brandish an appropriate club and mime the strangling of serpents so that a physical comedy is put in motion in preparation for the anti-climax of his exit. The boy might attempt to obey the order with absurd dignity or he could ignore it and run away until safely out of sight.

Between the heroes, the actors who represent them, and the on-stage audience, members of the theatre audience can choose to whom they give most attention and in whom they take most pleasure. Earlier in the play they will have given sympathy or, at least, alert attention to the four pairs of lovers as their stories develop and move towards a conclusion in which they would all be at peace with each other. Now, however, when these lovers have become an on-stage audience, they mock and deflate the well-meaning actors who are attempting to present the mighty Worthies and the audience in the theatre is liable to find them insensitive or positively cruel. When that is their reaction, attention will turn to the amateur actors as they manage to 'keep some state' in their performance or cast off pretence and express their own feelings openly.

The ancient, impoverished, romantic, and absurd Spanish knight Don Adriano de Armado seems to have been borrowed from Cervantes' *History of the Valorous and Witty Knight Errant, Don Quixote* but that parody of romantic epics was not published until 1604, years after Shakespeare had created his own errant and would-be

valorous knight. Armado has the task of presenting the
Worthies to their audience but does so by speaking aside
to the king and giving him a paper that names the nine
heroes, who will be represented by four actors. Although
hearing only Armado's opening words, the Princess immediately takes the lead in criticism by remarking that he
'speaks not like a man of God his making'. Armado
replies immediately – 'That is all one, my fair, sweet,
honey monarch' – before hinting that problems have
indeed been encountered and wishing for a contented
audience:

> I protest, the schoolmaster is exceeding fantastical; too
> too vain, too too vain; but we will put it, as they say, to
> *fortuna de la guerra*. I wish you the peace of mind, most
> royal couplement!
>
> (V.ii.526–31)

Armado leaves the stage and the King is left to read out
details of the pageant's cast and announce the players'
entry: 'The ship is under sail, and here she comes amain'
(l. 542). With this image the King recognizes the actors'
confidence and pride, and at the same time, in an age
when people were very dependent on changeable sea-
winds, alludes to the inevitable risk that they take.
Although from the start the theatre audience is invited
to laugh at the amateur actors, Shakespeare has ensured
that good intentions and failure become more evident
than parody in their performance.

When Armado's turn comes to face an interruption,
and he does so with more dignity than the others,
Shakespeare introduces an unforeseen event that takes
all the wind out of the pageant's sails. At this point
Costard announces that Jaquenetta is two months pregnant and that the 'child brags in her belly' it is Armado's.
Immediately performance is forgotten and a quarrel
breaks out between the knight and the clown, who has
also been courting the 'country wench'. Threatened with
being 'infamonize[d] ... among potentates' (ll. 667–8),
Armado issues a challenge only to find that his honour is

put still further at risk. When Costard strips to the waist in order to slash at his rival with a sword, he repeatedly refuses to follow his lead as the rules of duelling decreed that he should. The performance of the pageant continues to be held up while Armado becomes increasingly embarrassed and progressively more polite. Finally, when Berowne asks the reason why he refuses to strip, the actor drops all pretence and gathering what dignity he can, confesses: 'The naked truth of it is: I have no shirt; I go woolward for penance' (ll. 697–8). Boyet, the professional courtier, increases the knight's embarrassment with a run of witticisms that accuse him of wearing Jaquenetta's dish-cloth next to his heart for a favour. By this time, the audiences on stage and in the theatre may both be laughing freely at Armado's expense; on other occasions or with different actors, laughter in the theatre will be stopped by sympathy for the knight. Then, at this moment of choice between two views of the stage, Shakespeare introduces yet another totally unexpected event that establishes yet another kind of illusion and another perspective on all that has come before. The contrast with parody could scarcely be greater when Marcade enters with news that the King of France, the princess's father, has died.[3]

Two circumstances are remarkable. First, the sudden clash between laughter and response to the fact of death. Although the announcement is swift and compact on the page, its fall-out is widespread on stage and continues to register. The sails of the entire comedy will have to be re-rigged for the sudden change of wind and performance is likely to stall before it can, once more, sail amain. Some actors may fail to find an appropriate transition for the persons they play and so add other failures to those that have been brought about while the ambitious pageant was being performed. It is also possible that both audiences will now be 'generous … gentle … [and] humble', as no one in the on-stage audience has been towards the theatrical débâcle. The second remarkable outcome is that Armado, after his own personal failure, now realizes that he is able to change. While his fellow actors are dispersing, he holds back to confess:

> For mine own part, I breathe free breath. I have seen the day of wrong through the little hole of discretion, and I will right myself like a soldier.
>
> (ll. 711–14)

In this comedy, failures in performance change the course of the play by revealing alternative views of persons and actions. '*The Pageant of the Worthies*' is far from being a parody when it establishes new values and deepens an audience's perception.

* * *

Don Armado wishes his audience 'peace of mind' and this is the gift that the failure of an ambitious pageant and the off-stage presence of death may bring about through a performance of *Love's Labour's Lost.* Such contentment will be hard-won, a consequence of both mockery and embarrassment, and not some anodyne or forgetful comfort. In *A Midsummer Night's Dream,* which followed shortly after (1595–6), the 'tedious brief scene' of '*Pyramus and Thisbe*' is more complex and more sustained as a performance, with the possibility of failure more continuously present. Nevertheless, Bottom and his fellow amateurs – 'hard-handed men that work in Athens here' (V.i.72) – are able to finish their play, hero and heroine dying as they think fit. These actors are more courageous than those in the earlier comedy. With an audience that is just as carping, they answer back freely and carry on with their performances regardless of criticism. Self-defence brings about the one spectacular defeat when Starveling, the tailor who presents Moonshine, is told that his performance is 'the greatest error of all' and makes his audience weary; his light is seen to be visibly 'in the wane'. Faced with outright disbelief, this actor loses patience, deserts his script, and answers criticism with blunt facts, probably being very hurt and very angry:

> All that I have to say is to tell you that the lanthorn is the moon; I, the Man i' th' Moon; this thorn-bush, my thorn-bush; and this dog, my dog.
>
> (V.i.239–53)

This fails to silence criticism but, fortunately for Starveling, Flute the bellows-mender does that for him by entering at this very moment in the role of Thisby. These actors were ready from the start to outface failure, as their leader, Peter Quince, boldly announces in the mispunctuated Prologue:

> If we offend, it is with our good will... .
>   All for your delight
> We are not here. That you should here repent you,
> The actors are at hand.
>
> (V.i.108 ff.)

This comedy is a parody in so far as it imitates and ridicules the interludes of several decades earlier. In those days a handful of actors would tour the country and set their plays in action on a simple stage, often announcing the persons or functions they will represent and explaining what is happening while they are doing it. Also parodied are the loaded, alliterative verse and calamitous, blood-soaked action of the first English translations and imitations of Seneca's tragedies. The Prologue summarizes what to expect and sets the tone:

> Anon comes Pyramus, sweet youth and tall,
> And finds his trusty Thisby's mantle slain;
> Whereat with blade, with bloody blameful blade,
> He bravely breach'd his boiling bloody breast ...
>
> (ll. 143ff.)

Sweet and *trusty*, mixed with the other bludgeoning words, do nothing to prevent the on-stage audience from commenting on the play's absurdities and the 'asses' who are performing it (ll. 151–3). When the love story, or 'very tragical mirth' (ll. 56–7), is coming to an end, parody extends to the simple words and out-right declarations of purpose that were found in Mummers' Plays and other folk entertainments. In Thisby's concluding 'passion', homely images taken from English country life are used inappropriately in emphatic verse which mixes the Fates of classical myth with the gore and 'trusty sword' of a slain knight from popular romances:

> These lily lips,
> This cherry nose,
> These yellow cowslip cheeks,
> Are gone, are gone;
> Lovers, make moan;
> His eyes were green as leeks.
> O Sisters Three,
> Come, come to me,
> With hands as pale as milk;
> Lay them in gore,
> Since you have shore
> With shears his thread of silk... .
>
> (ll. 315ff.)

Heroic endeavour and passionate feeling are expressed here in simple and repetitive language that would be appropriate if Shakespeare were writing a parody, but they are ridiculed in such a way that a theatre audience is able to respond freely and generously to Thisby's predicament. She elicits sympathy by virtue of unaffected, sensuous epithets and, probably, by the serious-minded efforts of a young and 'homespun' actor to live up to the demands of the mythic story and carry it to its blood-stained conclusion. Laughter at the muddled descriptions and preposterous rhetoric can relax the mind and encourage a bond between spectators and performer so that mockery is dissipated or entirely dissolved in an alternative and affecting view of the play.

In this later comedy, Shakespeare kept the on-stage audience more continuously active and in focus than for *Love's Labours Lost.* Even before the actors have begun, the Master of Revels had given them little chance of success:

PHILOSTRATE   I have heard it over,
   And it is nothing, nothing in the world;
   Unless you can find sport in their intents,
   Extremely stretch'd and conn'd with cruel pain
   To do you service.

(V.i.77–81)

A debate follows, with Duke Theseus prepared to be sympathetic to 'tongue-tied simplicity' and his bride, Hyppolita, not wishing to see 'wretchedness o'ercharged / And duty in his service perishing' (ll. 104–5, 85–6). During the performance, response from the on-stage audience varies between incredulity, impatience, dismissive criticism, and perverse pleasure. The theatre audience can laugh either at the drama-within-the-comedy and the efforts of its actors, or at the laboured puns, self-evident observations, and personalized insults that the stage audience makes from its position of detached superiority. Theseus points out how much depends on an audience:

HIPPOLYTA   This is the silliest stuff that ever I heard.
THESEUS   The best in this kind are but shadows; and
   the worst are no worse, if imagination amend them.
HIPPOLYTA   It must be your imagination then, and not
   theirs.
THESEUS   If we imagine no worse of them than they of
   themselves, they may pass for excellent men. Here
   come two noble beasts in, a man and a lion.

(ll. 209–15)

As the actors work their way through the play, individual spectators change their opinions. At one moment, Hyppolita confesses sympathy for Pyramus – 'Beshrew my heart, but I pity the man' (ll. 282) – but soon she is 'aweary' of Moon, even though he shines 'with a good grace'. Just before the end, when her own wedding night approaches and Pyramus is dead, she hopes that Thisby's speech will be brief. What is constant is neither the reactions of the on-stage audience nor the effectiveness of the play within the play, but the actors' commitment and courage in acting their roles: this offers the theatre audience their own, alternative view of the entire play.

When Pyramus and Thisby are both dead and after two more particularly pointless comments from the young lovers watching on stage, Bottom rises from his pretended death to offer further entertainment in the form of either an Epilogue or a boisterous Bergomask. The dance is chosen and a silence begins to be established: the on-stage audience makes no further comment and, when their encore is over, the actors leave without another word. Everyone will have heard 'the iron tongue of midnight' (l. 352), which summons the lovers to their marriage beds and allows a troop of uninhibited fairies to take over the stage. Theseus assumes charge of the ending with a last reference to the 'palpable-gross play' that has 'well beguil'd / The heavy gait of night'. Then he, like everyone else, falls silent as he leaves with Hippolyta. While members of the theatre audience watch the silent emptying of the stage, any thoughts put into words will be their own until Puck enters to announce the darkness of night, with its ominous sounds and long memories:

> Now the hungry lion roars,
> And the wolf behowls the moon;
> Whilst the heavy ploughman snores,
> All with weary task fordone.
> Now the wasted brands do glow,
> Whilst the screech-owl, screeching loud,
> Puts the wretch that lies in woe
> In remembrance of a shroud... .

Puck is a 'sprite' and self-styled 'merry wanderer of the night' (II.i.33, 43) and he alone remains on stage after

the fairies have entered and blessed the house. In taking
leave of the theatre audience he invites those who have
been 'offended' by the performances to consider the
play a 'weak and idle theme, / No more yielding but a
dream' (V.i.412–17). Puck is under-selling the pleasures
on offer since a generous, gentle and humble response is
also possible and the more likely. By introducing what
seems like a parody of the theatre's presentation of love,
fate, and death, Shakespeare has laid bare the basis of
any theatrical event. A play's success is precarious
because it depends on actors undertaking roles that take
them out of their usual selves and on an audience accepting its fiction when they hardly know their own minds
and are affected by other events than those represented
in the play. Failure to create an illusion that holds an audience's attention is a recurrent danger in theatre for
which neither play-text, staging, performance, nor audience bears all the responsibility. The audience always has
a choice to make between sharing the feelings and values
enacted on stage and preferring others that arise in their
own minds in reaction to the performance.

By placing a 'tedious brief scene … [of] very tragical
mirth' as the climactic and concluding event of *A
Midsummer Night's Dream* (V.i.56–7), Shakespeare has extended the comedy's scope by multiplying the focus of attention. As the 'homespun' actors persevere with the
roles they play before an often hostile audience, a theatre
audience may experience a 'peace of mind' that is mysteriously revealing about their own aspirations and endeav-
ours, as if the play has been the most haunting of dreams,
not any ordinary one.

* * *

Theatre is hospitable to parody because exaggerated
performance comes all too easily and mimicry is a gift
that many actors possess. Failure is also well known, not
at all funny or intentional but arising whenever actors
are unable to hold attention or achieve credibility.

Shakespeare sometimes used all these propensities by positively encouraging falsity and then exposing its shortcomings by contrast with what is more true, instinctive, or compelling. This affects the reception of an entire play because when choosing to believe one aspect of performance rather than another, an audience becomes closer and more attached to what seems to be truly present on stage. Study of a text should at these times take a double view so that the reader grasps all that is happening on stage.

As You Like It (1599/1600) is the third comedy that Shakespeare set for the most part in the open countryside where it could be free from the procedures and expectations of day-to-day living. By developing earlier devices, many different performances are presented to jostle with each other while on-stage audiences comment on their success or failure. By these means, members of a theatre audience are prompted to make up their own, perhaps equally varied, minds. There is no play within this play to parody performance and provide a distorted reflection of the main action, as in *Love's Labour's Lost* or *A Midsummer Night's Dream*. The double view is established by questions that on-stage spectators ask about behaviour and truthfulness, by contrasts arising when the play's action switches between several more or less independent stories, and by spoken accounts of events that happen off stage. And, more effective than all these devices, moments of failure are used to direct attention to its causes and alert the theatre audience to anticipate consequences.

The stage is crowded for the first time when Duke Frederick and his court assemble for a contest between an amateur challenger and Charles, the professional wrestler. Off stage the latter has just thrown three brothers in quick succession, leaving little hope of their survival; their old father and 'all the beholders' are said to be weeping (I.ii.110–15). Charles is now to be opposed by 'the youth' Orlando, whom the audience has already seen being treated shamefully and tyrannically by an older brother – for he also is one of three sons. The match will be watched by Celia and Rosalind, daughters of the present duke and the now banished Duke Senior, which leads Touchstone the fool to comment that this was 'the first time that ever I heard breaking of ribs was sport for ladies' (ll. 122–3). Before and during the contest, the two young women make clear whom they support and, when it proves to be Charles who is thrown and has to be carried off stage unable to speak, they go to congratulate Orlando. Duke Frederick leaves the scene without rewarding the victor, on the grounds that his father had been a loyal friend of the banished duke, and then, after this rebuff, Orlando finds himself face to face with Rosalind, daughter of that duke, and it is his turn to be speechless, not in defeat but in wonder. Neither of them is fully in charge of what is happening between them and this failure, shown in awkwardness and hesitation, encourages the theatre audience to think beyond and ahead of what is being said. The wrestling match has functioned, in this respect, like the play-within-the-play in the two earlier comedies but to a less comic and judgemental effect that suits the beginning, rather than the end, of a play.

Once the action moves to the Forest of Arden for Act II, scene i, different forms of spectator-sport follow one after another, each calling for more than one kind of response. The first scene starts with Duke Senior telling his 'co-mates and brothers in exile' that, by finding 'good in everything', he has learnt to enjoy a sequestered life amongst trees, brooks, and stones (ll. 1–18). From among his audience, Amiens compliments him on the ability to translate 'the stubbornness of fortune / Into so quiet and so sweet a style' but already the Duke has lost confidence in what he has said and proposes that they should all join together in the sport of hunting deer. But this does not satisfy him either and he says so, before anyone can respond:

> Come, shall we go and kill us venison?
> And yet it irks me the poor dappled fools,
> Being native burghers of this desert city,

Should, in their own confines, with forked heads
Have their round haunches gor'd.

(II.i.21–5)

That gives a cue for an anonymous Lord to report that
'the melancholy Jaques' has been seen watching a
wounded stag that stands 'on th' extremest verge of the
swift brook, / Augmenting it with tears'. The Duke's attention is caught at once and, having asked if Jaques had,
as usual, 'moralize[d] this spectacle', he is told a narrative in which direct quotation gives the speaker scope for
impersonation. Hearing that Jaques has called the
foresters 'usurpers, tyrants, and what's worse' because
they hunt and kill the deer in their 'assign'd and native
dwelling-place' (ll. 24–63), the Duke's enthusiastic response is to go and see for himself: 'I love to cope him in
these sullen fits, / For then he's full of matter' (ll. 67–8).
After the wrestling with its sudden consequences, this
scene offers a number of self-conscious performances
and thoughtful responses. Then everyone leaves the
stage in search of new entertainment.

Another series of performances begins with the entry of
Celia, disguised as Aliena, a shepherdess, and Rosalind, disguised as her beautiful young brother Ganymede. They
arrive together in Arden, along with Touchstone, the
'clownish fool' (I.iii.16). Weary in body and spirit, none of
them is happy in their chosen roles; Rosalind says as much,
finding 'in her heart to disgrace [her] man's apparel' by
crying 'like a woman'. But entertainment is at hand with
the entry of 'a young man and an old in solemn talk' about
the follies, fantasies, and pains of being in love:

>   … if thou hast not sat as I do now,
> Wearing thy hearer in thy mistress' praise,
> Thou hast not lov'd;
> Or if thou hast not broke from company
> Abruptly, as my passion now makes me,
> Thou hast not lov'd.
> O Phebe, Phebe, Phebe!   *Exit.*

(II.iv.34–40)

When Silvius is unable to continue and so gets up and runs off stage calling out his mistress's name, a theatre audience will almost certainly laugh at him while on stage each person responds to the spectacle in a different way. Rosalind is caught up in her own recent experience: 'Alas, poor shepherd! searching of thy wound, / I have by hard adventure found mine own.' Touchstone reflects on past times, when he had courted Jane Smile and was left 'wooing of a peascod instead of her'; as he remembers his own tears, he breaks off to make verbal jokes and philosophize about mortality. Celia says nothing at all about Silvius's predicament but calls on the others to find some food: she is fainting 'almost to death', as the others would be if what they were watching left them leisure to think about hunger. With these practicalities now in mind, Touchstone makes contact with Corin, the older shepherd, and Rosalind, putting on a better performance as Ganymede, negotiates the purchase of a vacant cottage. Celia revives and they all go off in search of shelter and nourishment. Actual need has displaced everything else in importance and a theatre audience, alerted to what sentiment fails to supply, is free to laugh and sympathize in whatever proportion they instinctively choose.

At the top of the next scene, Jaques makes his first entry to the play. He has already been talked about and the Duke has gone off to seek his company and yet now he is silent among another on-stage audience that listens to Amiens singing about the pleasures of rustic life:

> Under the greenwood tree
> Who loves to lie with me,
> And turn his merry note
> Unto the sweet bird's throat,
> Come hither, come hither, come hither.
> Here shall he see
> No enemy
> But winter and rough weather.

(II.v.1–8)

More foresters may be present than the '*two or three*' of the Folio's stage direction for the previous scene because

Charles had reported that 'many young gentlemen flock
to [the banished Duke] every day, and fleet the time
carelessly, as they did in the golden world' (I.i.106–9).
Amiens' song celebrates this gathering of carefree exiles
but after one verse Jaques asks for another to feed his
own discordant mood:

> JAQUES More, more, I prithee, more.
> AMIENS It will make you melancholy, Monsieur Jaques.
> JAQUES I thank it. More, I prithee, more. I can suck
> melancholy out of a song, as a weasel sucks eggs.
> More, I prithee, more.
>
> (II.v.9–13)

Eventually Amiens sings a concluding stanza in the same
vein:

> Who doth ambition shun,
> And loves to live i' th' sun,
> Seeking the food he eats,
> And pleas'd with what he gets,
> Come hither, come hither, come hither;
> Here shall he see, etc.
>
> (ll. 34–9)

The Folio text does not repeat the whole chorus but at the
start of the new stanza it has a stage direction, '*Altogether
here*', so that the entertainment ends with the shared pleasure of choral singing, from which Jaques sets himself
apart. He supplies a further stanza that was 'made yester-
day' and offers an alternative view of their predicament:

> If it do come to pass
> That any man turn ass,
> Leaving his wealth and ease
> A stubborn will to please,
> Ducdame, ducdame, ducdame;
> Here shall he see
> Gross fools as he,
> An if he will come to me.
>
> (ll. 46–53)

Asked what *ducdame* means, Jaques says it is 'a Greek in-vocation, to call fools into a circle': which is just what has happened to the on-stage audience as it gathers around to hear him read the new stanza. No one says anything to that and there is no more singing: the inter-lude deflates suddenly, perhaps to uneasy laughter. Jaques walks off alone, declaring no more positive in-tention than to sleep or to 'rail against all the first-born of Egypt' (ll. 57–8). Amiens also goes off to tell the ban-ished duke that his banquet is prepared, his on-stage audience following. This musical interlude does nothing to advance any of the several narratives in the play and it leaves a theatre audience to find its own re-sponse to Jaques's misanthropy and scorn for con-tented, communal idleness. Since this role will attract the most experienced and effective actor in any theatre company, Jaques is able to gain attention even in com-petition with the singing of a male chorus. A theatre au-dience is likely to have seen everything 'with a parted eye'[4] and its members once more find themselves left to choose where their individual interests and sympathies should lie.

These three interludes are examples of the many vari-eties of audience–play relationships that are presented on stage in this comedy. Together they strengthen a theatre audience's independence of mind and encourage the thought that all is valued according to how it is viewed – in other words, 'as you like it'. By itself this is little more than an everyday observation but in a performance of this play the perception arises freshly, as if on its own voli-tion, out of many different sensations that range from country pleasures to 'hard adventure', from forgotten memories to momentary surprises, from reactions to everyday happenings, and from unusual and demanding encounters with tyranny, banishment, and death. As a theatre audience is progressively engaged with the play, its awareness complicates and deepens. And these per-ceptions can survive after the end of a performance because they have become rooted in each spectator's in-dividual and independent responses. Recognition of this process is crucial for an understanding of many moments in the play-text and its entire theatrical life.

* * *

Twice, the action of *As You Like It* is called a *pageant*, that is, a show to be enjoyed and thought about, as '*The Pageant of the Worthies*' in *Love's Labour's Lost* was meant to be. By this time Shakespeare had developed the device so that it no longer needed the performance of a scripted play that is watched by an on-stage audience: performances, conscious and unconscious, occur as if spontaneously throughout the comedy. By turns they are daring, necessary, fanciful, comic, and serious. Some persons who watch on stage sympathize while others laugh or ridicule those who are performing.

The first pageant has multiple *dramatis personae* and is presented in a speech by Jaques after the Duke, in his philosophizing mood, has reflected that 'This wide and universal theatre / Presents more woeful pageants than the scene / Wherein we play' (II.vii.137–9). Accepting the cue, Jaques proceeds to evoke the seven acts of a man's life, using the words and, probably, the voice and behaviour that are appropriate to each one of them in turn. His performance is so impressive that no one comments on stage, everyone being held by its eloquence, wit and credibility. Yet as he concludes, the theatre audience is given visual evidence that his presentation does not always reflect the facts of life. At this very moment Orlando re-enters carrying the ancient Adam, and Jaques's description of man's last Act as a 'second childishness and mere oblivion; / Sans teeth, sans eyes, sans taste, sans every thing' (ll. 139–66) can no longer be accepted as the whole and invariable truth. Plain for all to see, Adam is still in possession of his faculties and still able to act out of loyalty to his old master's son.

The other 'pageant' is played after Orlando fails to return when he promised and so causes Rosalind to fear that he is 'not true in love'. Celia does not help matters by mocking Rosalind's anxiety and declaring that 'all's brave that youth mounts and folly guides' (III.iv.23–41). At just this moment, Corin calls them both to witness 'a pageant truly play'd / Between the pale complexion of true love / And the red glow of scorn and proud disdain' (ll. 47–9). What they see moments later would be a parody of conventional courtship if Phebe and Silvius intended any humour as they work their way through a gamut of similes and postures taken from the poetry of hopeless love, or if Shakespeare had provided speeches for the on-stage audience that prompted mockery or laughter. Instead of the latter, Rosalind is soon seriously involved in the drama on Silvius's behalf, speaking to Phebe with contrasting brashness:

> Down on your knees,
> And thank heaven, fasting, for a good man's love;
> For I must tell you friendly in your ear:
> Sell when you can; you are not for all markets.
>   (III.v.57–60)

This further cue for the theatre audience to laugh puts Rosalind's warning to Silvius into a wider perspective: ''Tis such fools as you / That makes the world full of ill-favour'd children' (III.v.52–3). Phebe's response is to fall in love with Rosalind's Ganymede:

> Sweet youth, I pray you chide a year together;
> I had rather hear you chide than this man woo.
>   (ll. 64–5)

When this player in the pageant herself becomes an on-stage audience for Rosalind, the action immediately changes course.

Consciously or unconsciously, the persons in this play will sometimes perform for their own or other people's benefit, sometimes seeming to parody themselves. All who read or hear Orlando's poems in praise of Rosalind mock them, and so does Rosalind when she realizes how others are responding. The forced rhymes and fanciful epithets of conventional love poetry have been wrenched into absurdities and then these efforts are topped by Touchstone's extemporary verses, which turn compliment into lewd and leering provocation (III.ii.78–112). In the poem that Rosalind had read out, simple statements became parodies by repetition, and soon after this, speaking for herself, *she* tries to express overwhelming feelings by means of repetition and absurdly far-fetched images, for example:

> O coz, coz, coz, my pretty little coz, that thou didst know how many fathom deep I am in love! But it cannot be sounded; my affection hath an unknown bottom, like the Bay of Portugal.
>
> (IV.i.184–7)

Rosalind is both player and attentive audience for her own performance. This provides no escape but has driven her forward to imagine herself:

> ... more jealous ... than a Barbary cock-pigeon over his hen, more clamorous than a parrot against rain, more new-fangled than an ape, more giddy in my desires than a monkey... .
>
> (IV.i.130–9)

Towards the end of the play, self-conscious performances become more sustained and elaborate. A forester who has killed a deer is dressed in the dead creature's hide and wears its horns in order to be presented to the Duke 'like a Roman conqueror' (IV.ii.3–4). Everyone on stage joins in the masquerade except Jaques, who calls for a song, 'no matter how it be in tune, so it make noise enough'. The Folio directs that '*the rest shall bear this burden*:'

> Take thou no scorn to wear the horn;
> It was a crest ere thou wast born.
>   Thy father's father wore it;
>   And thy father bore it.

> The horn, the horn, the lusty horn,
> Is not a thing to laugh to scorn.

No one comments on stage, so that the theatre audience is left to welcome or look away from the sight of the animal's bloody skin. The sound of noisy triumph is bound to draw attention but the song's verbal jokes may be variously received, as cruel or sexist boasting, apology, or an instinctive expression of communal happiness.

Response to performance is often unexpected. When Touchstone meets William, a natural or 'simple' clown who is his rival for Audrey's love, he threatens to kill him and acts as if he were both a ruthless swordsman and an official of the law. William says or does nothing in response, until he is told to 'tremble, and depart', and, even then, he waits for Audrey to encourage him before he leaves, bidding 'God rest you merry, sir' (V.i.37–55), as if Touchstone's threats had failed to register. When two pages sing about the pleasure that lovers find in a cornfield in spring time, Touchstone listens with Audrey in silence as if in agreement. Only when the song is finished are the boys told that their singing was 'untuneable' and 'foolish' (V.iii.32–7), so that they go off protesting and, probably, puzzled. After Touchstone's highly skilled performance as swordsman and courtier in the final scene, to which the Duke and Jaques respond (see above pp. 13–16), Hymen enters and immediately draws everyone's attention by proclaiming that 'mirth in heaven' will follow the wedding vows (V.iv.102–4). At this impressive and unexpected entry, the entire on-stage audience is speechless.

This comedy's pastoral setting, performances, and on-stage audiences offer many perspectives to the theatre audience as the action moves from one centre of attention to another. The several strands of narrative are clear for all to see but how the play is viewed is constantly changing. Members of a theatre audience are invited to take the 'greenwood' world as they 'like it' and are given some clues to the world that the persons of the play have left behind. When the actor of Rosalind returns to curtsey and speak an Epilogue, members of the theatre audience are encouraged to think twice about the performance and speculate about personal relationships in the world to which they are about to return.

* * *

In the comedies Shakespeare created a double view of the stage by means of plays-within-plays and their unmanageable audiences, by many instinctive, self-conscious, or failed performances, and by responses that go along with a performance or cut across it with disbelief. He provided a multiple dramatic focus by these means and developed a rapid and increasingly sensitive control over the many elements that make up a complete theatrical event. Each comedy has a central scene where a divided focus is of paramount importance: Portia and Nerissa pretending to be a lawyer and his clerk; Benedick and then Beatrice being deceived by the not entirely convincing performances of their well-wishers; Malvolio 'practising behaviour' while Sir Toby and his companions laugh at his efforts. A theatre audience watching *The Taming of the Shrew* will often see that both Petruchio and Katharine are performing, and may do so more quickly than their various on-stage audiences. The many variations of a double view of the stage helped to establish Shakespeare's characteristic mode of comedy, and although seldom as obvious in operation, a similar presentation is found in both the histories and were tragedies.

It is most evident in sustained speeches delivered before a potentially active crowd, much like the plays-within-plays of the comedies: for example, the deposition scene in *Richard the Second*; the funeral orations of Brutus and Mark Antony in *Julius Caesar*; two very different speeches to the Senators in the third scene of *Othello*; Claudius's address to the court in the second scene of *Hamlet* – the central scene of this tragedy has the performance and reception of '*The Murder of Gonzago*', which is still more reminiscent of the comedies. The titular hero of *Richard the Third*, Edmund in *King Lear*, and Iago in *Othello* are repeatedly shown as actors performing or preparing to perform. When Richard, as yet Duke of Gloucester, acts as if fighting for his life '*in rusty armour*,' an on-stage audience stubbornly refuses to respond as he intended, but, despite an incredible role, he is more successful when pretending to be a holy man and standing between two bishops (III.v and vii). Although less clearly signalled than in the earliest comedies, these performances and their audiences have a similarly pervasive effect; when these actors meet with failure the result is more unsettling.

Before peace is sealed at the end of *Henry the Fifth*, King Henry tries to persuade the French princess, Katherine, to be his bride by posing as a 'plain king' and a 'plain soldier' while struggling with her imperfect understanding of English and his own incompetence in her language. His long speech is received in silence until he offers 'a good heart' and begs for a response. Eventually, comes the self-evident and hardly unexpected, 'Is it possible dat I sould love de enemy of France?' (V.ii.168–9). He still persists in trying to present himself favourably, speaking with ever greater directness while acknowledging, 'I shall never move thee in French, unless it be to laugh at me' (ll. 185–6). After he has failed several times in the role of lover, she agrees to do 'as it shall please de roi mon père' (ll. 243–4), upon which he tries to kiss her hand, only to be stopped when told that to permit this would be against the custom in France for unmarried ladies. Again he persists and, promising to do so 'patiently and yielding', he is at last able to kiss her on the mouth. She says nothing and it is he who responds, with words that can imply satisfaction, pleasure, wonder, or perhaps, submission: 'You have witchcraft in your lips, Kate' (ll. 271–2). The separation caused by ignorance of each other's language and the presence of a chaperone has converted what was intended to be a duologue into a solo performance in the face of uneasy, and some hostile, responses. The theatre audience is left to judge how heart-felt and mutual is the consent that everyone on stage assumes when Katherine's father returns soon after they have kissed. The response of a theatre audience will depend on how the actors have played their parts here and throughout the play and on any predisposition in favour of one of the performers that individual spectators may have brought with them to the theatre. This wooing-scene, with its double view of the stage and repeated failures in communication, is so placed in the play's action that it leads to the conclusion of the central story. The doubts it can raise among a theatre audience about the quality of performance and credibility of words will affect the reception of the play's themes concerning ambition, nationhood, kingship, politics, service, warfare, and suffering, and its final moments in which peace is declared between the two warring nations.

In Shakespeare's plays, performances are presented that meet with many degrees of success and failure. At one extreme, the First Player's delivery of Aeneas' speech to Dido about the horrors of war is so convincing that Hamlet waits until he is alone before responding fully and personally to the experience. The other extreme of failure occurs far more frequently in the tragedies, as exemplified in Lear's many attempts to be a powerful king and loving father. In the first scene, the composition and composure of a public occasion at first divides speakers from spectators as the performance of a play can divide actors from audience. In contrast with her sisters' compliant responses to their father's formal question about their love for him, Cordelia's asides ignore that barrier and her unexpected 'Nothing' as the measure of her love disturbs every other performance and threatens a comprehensive failure. When the Earl of Kent intervenes on Cordelia's behalf, formality is succeeded by violence as Lear loses self-control in 'hideous rashness' and draws his sword. Albany and Cornwall cease to be silent observers and enter the action for the first time, urging 'Dear sir, forbear' (l. 161). Although Lear reasserts his 'potency' with a solemn oath, the banished Kent steps outside the main action and speaks his mind freely before he leaves. The response of a theatre audience is likely to change several times in the course of the scene; even its view of Cordelia's strength of mind and restraint in speech can become uncertain, at least momentarily.

Among Goneril's household in Act I, scene iv, the fool makes his first appearance as a highly self-conscious performer. Some of his jokes are received in silence by the king who is his principal audience, and it is left to Kent, now disguised as the serving-man Caius, to respond in his place. But Fool insists on being heard by his master, provoking Lear to ask questions and twice to threaten punishment with a whip (ll. 109, 179). At other times, for a brief moment, this performer and his chosen audience seem to be of one mind: at one point, he asks Lear to 'stand' by his side and, when he does, the fool calls the king a fool (ll. 139–49). When Goneril enters they both, one after another, react to her presence before she says a word. Eventually gaining silence, she condemns all who are present, her father, the fool, and the numerous knights who have gone along with the entertainment, probably laughing at jokes that are broad and dangerous enough to encourage the 'rank and not-to-be-endured riots' that Goneril denounces (ll. 200–2). Lear seems to lose all sense of what is happening or else puts on a performance that uses, as we have seen (p. 142, above), only the simplest of words: 'Are you our daughter?' he asks; and more pointed still, 'Does any here know me? This is not Lear. / ... Who is it that can tell me who I am?' (ll. 217–29). Before long, gathering his strength once more and with no hint of performance, he cries out 'Darkness and devils' and calls for his horses to be saddled. Driven now by contrasting impulses, he remembers the pain Cordelia had caused him, curses Goneril, calls 'Away, Away!' and, before leaving the scene, weeps and promises to 'resume the shape which thou dost think / I have cast off for ever' (ll. 300–10). By this time, the Duke of Albany, Goneril's husband, has entered and his concern at what he sees is very different from Goneril's firm rejection of her father and Lear's equally firm rejection of his daughter: 'Pray, sir, be patient... . Now, gods that we adore, whereof comes this?' (ll. 261, 290). Even at this moment when feelings of love and hatred are highly enflamed and unmistakable, Shakespeare has established another view on what is happening that will prompt a theatre audience to question who is most responsible for the violent passions, and who might have the greatest ability to influence events. Another jolt to the audience's perception follows when attention is drawn to Fool, who has been forgotten by Lear and left behind: earlier he had commanded his master's attention; now he has failed to perform and is too frightened as a spectator to follow him until he is ordered to do so.

At Gloucester's castle, confronted by both Regan and Goneril, Lear is forced to ask for ever-smaller favours. Having struggled against his tears and begged the heavens to give him patience, he stops acting like a king and accepts that he is 'a poor old man, / As full of grief as age; wretched in both' (II.iv.271–2). But performing this role does not satisfy him and, almost at once, he asks the gods for 'noble anger', threatening revenge on both daughters. Then this role, like the last, cannot be sustained and words and thoughts both fail him:

> No, you unnatural hags,
> I will have such revenges on you both
> That all the world shall – I will do such things –
> What they are yet I know not; but they shall be
> The terrors of the earth. You think I'll weep.
> No, I'll not weep. *Storm and tempest.*
> I have full cause of weeping; but this heart
> Shall break into a hundred thousand flaws
> Or ere I'll weep. O Fool, I shall go mad!
> *Exeunt Lear, Gloucester, Kent, Fool.*

To find a receptive audience Lear turns to the fool, who has said nothing since the entrance of Regan some hundred and fifty lines earlier; in many performances, he is now clinging to his master. But Fool says nothing in response and neither does anyone else among those who follow the king off stage. Both Lear's terrifying anger and his humiliation are brought to the theatre audience's attention as his words begin to buckle with mental and physical failure.

Each scene involving Lear gives a double view so that an audience is drawn into the narrative and experiences its uncertainties on its own terms. As the action moves successively to the open heath, the interior of a hovel, and the beach at Dover where, eventually, Cordelia's soldiers find him, Lear attempts to understand and be understood. He draws close to the young Edgar who is performing as a mad beggar, to Kent in disguise as his serving-man, and, most intimately, to Gloucester after he has become a blind victim. He also responds to the increasingly terrified Fool, until this one-time companion, counsellor, and performer mysteriously disappears. In later movements of the story, Lear is almost helpless while Cordelia cares for him and he is silent when she prepares to fight a battle on his behalf. Not until they have both been captured and are on their way to prison does he command her attention once more, with tender and eloquent words. Finally, when she is dead and he is dying, Lear struggles to be understood although he is now barely able to speak. *The Tragedy of King Lear* is astonishingly varied in its treatment of performers and their on-stage audiences and so draws a theatre audience to probe behind appearances and respond in its own way as best it can.

Shakespeare's plays do not set up any hero as a model or recommend any doctrine or policy but they encourage spectators to become participants by questioning the truth or effectiveness of what is said and done. In the words of Don Armado, having looked 'through the little hole of discretion', they may then leave the theatre 'breathing free air' and enjoying an unusual 'peace of mind'.

* * *

When manipulating dramatic action to ensure a double view of the stage, Shakespeare's invention seems to have been inexhaustible as if drawing on a deep source of his creative instinct.

The concept of life as a 'wide and universal theatre' seems to underlie much of his writing in ways more subtle than those that Jaques expounds in As You Like It *(II.vii.137). An audience is repeatedly made aware that the persons of a play are performing with varying degrees of credibility and that, at other times, they speak a 'plain' truth and act in 'good faith'. When a person fails to perform in a chosen role, the laughter or disparaging response of an on-stage audience will often spur the theatre audience to do the same, or to take pity on the unsuccessful performer. In many ways and at moments of obvious importance in the narrative, alternative views of the dramatic action unsettle an audience's attitude by offering clues to unspoken motives or prompting disbelief, misgiving, or closer sympathy. This chapter has investigated the operation of double vision in a number of plays, and further study will discover similar devices in other plays that will help in evaluating both their themes and persons.*

Notes

1. See above, pp. 70–4 and 82–3.
2. The two texts are printed in parallel in the Regents Renaissance Drama Series, ed. J. W. Lever (Lincoln: University of Nebraska Press, 1971), from which the play is quoted here: V.i.221–2.
3. On the effect of this, see above, pp. 89–90.
4. The phrase is from *A Midsummer Night's Dream*, IV.i.186–7.

8

Criticism: Making the Plays One's Own

In much the same way as any natural phenomenon, a theatrical performance can appeal to the senses without being consciously understood.[1] Even a play's most literary qualities – its narrative, structure, language, imagery, its imitation of ordinary speech, and subtextual suggestions – co-exist in an audience's mind with a sensory experience. Words that are spoken do not function alone but always together with the individual and unique presence of the actors who speak them. All that happens in performance, visible to everyone in the theatre, will supplement and modify whatever a dramatist sets down on paper. Shakespeare was so aware of the physical, temporal, and actor-centred nature of performance that a play may be said to have danced in his mind as he wrote and imagined its more than ordinary existence on a stage. This book has tried to study that dazzling phenomenon and used various ways of grasping this complex and essentially theatrical art. The next step is to assess the consequences of this form of study.

* * *

In all theatrical events, three elements are involved: one or more persons perform; they are watched by other persons; and both parties share the same passage of time.

All these constituents affect whatever Shakespeare's plays become in performance and each one must, therefore, enter into any critical account of a play's stage-worthiness and the experience it offers audiences. Careful study of the text is a necessary and constant part of this but will not be sufficient on its own. A play's reflection and transformation of lived experience will depend not only on what is spoken but also on everything done on stage, and on the actors' physical beings, their skills, life-experiences, and imaginations. The time and place of performance, the nature and shape of the theatre, and the audience's response to all that happens as it develops during the course of the play, will all affect what becomes of the play-script and the experience it offers.

Shakespeare's plays are so responsive to all the variables of a theatrical event that little of permanent value can be learnt from any one visit to a theatre. Seeing the same production several times will demonstrate how each performance is different and how this modifies the effectiveness and meanings of the text. What is hesitant on one occasion can seem necessary and compelling on another. Simple words are sometimes surprising in effect and complex words may present little difficulty. Actions as well as words change their recognizable meanings and the focus of attention may not always be the same. If we see the same production on two occasions some months apart we will bring different expectations and concerns to the theatre and this will also modify our response. Through many theatre visits, however, we will discover that some basic features of a play are resistant to change. The shape and progress of its action – the 'plot' of the play, as Elizabethans would say[2] – will always remain constant and influence every moment. And usually some encounters prove able to hold attention no matter how they are played or how the words are spoken. On the other hand, if we see the same actor in the same role on different occasions we will find that certain speeches, some short phrases, and a few single words invite variations in meaning or emphasis while others have a constant and crucial significance. By experimenting with theatregoing in these ways we will learn to read a text theatrically, not only as a series of words to which we give meaning.

When seeing a play in performance is not practicable or affordable, or when a production is not worth much attention, theatre visits can be supplemented in many ways. For most Shakespeare plays, films, CDs and DVDs are available and, from time to time, the better known can be seen on television. These provide good ways of seeing the physical consequences of speaking a text and experiencing the changing nature of its action. By sharpening our view of performance, the camera and micro-technology have revealed aspects and implications of the texts that we might otherwise have missed. They can also sustain attention and build an emotional charge. Comparison of two film versions is an effective way of raising questions about interpretation, casting, performance, visual setting, stage business, and the effect of some crucial words. But even the most imaginative and responsive film is no substitute for theatregoing because its performances have been captured once and for all by the camera and are viewed without the participation of an audience. The action is seen only as the camera records and shows it, with some small details greatly exaggerated and many aspects lost to view. The spectator does not watch the play unfold in one unchanging space or share the consecutive minutes of the actors' performances. Nothing can be observed in any of the lens media without technical and editorial interference. The actors do not have a continuous experience of playing a text and an audience is not present at any moment of creation or fulfilment. No actor's physical presence is a continuous and palpable element in the performance as it is in a theatre. An individual viewer is unlikely to share the experience with other members of an audience so that responses are neither buoyed up nor challenged as they are among a crowded theatre audience. Although film images are taken from reality, once processed into their final form they cannot give the impression that the entire play is palpably happening in the here and now. For all its fluidity and finesse, as a social and topical event and as a spur to an audience's own imaginative creativity, the losses of cinematic art are very great, and these are among the most distinctive effects of Shakespeare's plays in performance. Because visual effects dominate the big screens and because a sound track heightens whatever the director has chosen to emphasize, the words of the text have a less dominant effect than when they are part of the performance of a company of actors and are followed by an audience that witnesses everything that is said and done on stage and is free to respond in its own ways.

Even our theatregoing will have limited use. The fully staged and carefully rehearsed productions of the present day offer a more controlled view of performance than those in Shakespeare's day, which were presented on an open stage, almost surrounded by an audience that sat or stood in the same light as the actors. This difference is increased when stage lighting is dramatically and sensitively varied and a soundtrack provided to accentuate the play's changing locations and moods. Despite new ways of controlling and concentrating attention, the actors we see are likely to be less dominant than in early performances and less free to respond to their audiences or the changing conditions and occasions of the staging. In exchange for these losses, contemporary scenographical and production techniques have brought the advantages of more suggestive settings for a play's action and a less distracted view of its more complex situations. If we wish to study the inherent nature of the plays in performance we need to look beyond the productions we happen to be able to see.

Looking at photographs of productions that are no longer being played can bring a sharper awareness of physical elements of Shakespeare's art.[3] Because these visual images come from times and places different from our own they can prompt us to notice implications of the texts that we would otherwise miss. When viewing Shakespeare's plays we must expect our usual reactions to be insufficient because the visual world and habits of seeing have changed since they were written. While we

can read books and consult dictionaries to learn about
the plays' language and ideas, only by visual evidence can
our sight be made more sensitive to many visual cues that
were once evident in the texts. Our expectations of what
the plays can offer will also be limited by the performances we have seen, and in this respect productions of
Shakespeare by companies from other cultures than our
own are an enlightening supplement to performances
and directorial styles that are found at home.[4] Some
foreign-language productions can seem more alive and
reveal more of the physical implications of the texts than
those in which words are readily understood. When we
are forced to look more closely to see what is happening
we can discover relationships, processes, and feelings that
escape attention when our minds are more at ease and
less in search of inner meanings and long-term consequences. A single physical image from a production in an
unknown language will sometimes seem so expressive
that it stays long in the memory.

Once we start being critical about our response
to Shakespeare's plays in performance, we will find
ourselves drawn to theatre companies that produce
contemporary plays in ways that are purposefully experi-
mental and reflect present-day life and consciousness.
Shakespeare could not have envisaged the technical
means in use today or many of the issues that particularly
concern us, but his sensibility and imagination extended
beyond the usual limits of his time. The very different impulses that we experience may sometimes find echoes in
his playscripts that more traditional productions are
unable to respect and embody. Divergent actions simultaneously presented, rapid shifts of consciousness and
dramatic focus, disembodied presences and instantaneous physical transformations, orchestrated and choreographed group activity, controlled and contained
violence, slow-motion action, sexual explicitness, topical
references, and close interface with an audience: all these
devices are found in recent theatre productions but are
seldom used in productions of Shakespeare. As we grow
familiar with them we will become more conscious of

elements of Shakespeare's imagination that may otherwise be lost to us.[5] A renewed emphasis on physicality in
performance, which is found in many productions of new
plays, could greatly assist in staging features of
Shakespeare's texts that are often ignored in production
or dismissed as merely fanciful or metaphoric: bodily
transformation or disappearance, sexual attraction experienced where least expected, a flower possessing magic
power, blood running so copiously that one could drown
in it, 'dogs of war' being unleashed, an entire world
disappearing or yielding to chaos.

Performances of Shakespeare's plays that are responsive to the reactions of their audiences offer the most
valuable support for theatrical study but these are not
often available. Some theatre companies offer educa-
tional workshops that are a useful alternative, especially
when experienced actors work on short passages of a text
to demonstrate how they can come alive in performance.
Another substitute would be an attempt to stage a play
ourselves. Although our skills and means are bound to be
rudimentary, the task is not so forbidding or unprofitable
as it might seem. Something of an audience's progressive
experience will be gained if a student simply reads an
entire play aloud, with no one hearing but with no break
in attention. A sense of a play's physical action can be discovered if the speeches of a single role are detached from
the text and spoken aloud from beginning to end with
the reader taking whatever time is needed to envisage
what is happening on stage as the lines are spoken. If a
group of people are gathered together and the roles of
one extended scene shared between them, the simplest
reading of the lines aloud will enable other features of a
play in performance to be encountered at first hand. The
text should then be memorized and the company meet
again to speak their lines and listen to each other, at first
simply standing together. If the readers take care to contrast with each other in pitch, tempo, volume, intention,
and feeling, the beginnings of a performance will bring
about changes of awareness and physical involvement.
Slowly, in this basic and very imperfect manner, the

speakers will begin to be actors and discover how the lines of dialogue can function and do their work in performance: how a momentary feeling begins to seem actual, how a person listens and responds without speaking, how one speech answers another, how words begin to seem necessary to the speaker, how timing seems crucial to sense and understanding. If a small audience can be gathered, its response will begin to affect performance and become part of the play's life. All this may need some bravado at first and a good deal of time, but patient, watchful work on a single scene will enable participants to experience some of the sensations and insights given by full and expert performances: a wider appreciation of a text's theatrical potential may be gained and, with good fortune, a chance of getting closer to the conditions in which Shakespeare envisaged his plays being staged.

Some actual encounter with the texts in performance is a necessary part of any study that respects the way in which they were written. Whether we are players, audience, or readers, this author allows us to take possession of his plays and make them, quite singularly, our own.

* * *

Theatregoing, theatre-making and theatrical study will, together, bring a critical awareness of many possible meanings that can arise in performance of one of Shakespeare's plays, rather than any single and definitive interpretation; and these discoveries will be in personal rather than authoritative terms.

Over the last fifty or so years, critics have become increasingly aware of the texts' unstable nature. Some have argued for multiple meanings or levels of meaning as more sources and analogues have been identified. By reading the texts in the light of a clearly stated idea or a specific aspect of social or personal life, other critics have identified a great number of 'issues' or 'arguments' in the plays that conflict with each other and range widely across conservative, revolutionary, occult, theological, metaphysical, and psychological opinions. Individually they have studied the texts as if looking at a wide landscape through a number of very narrow windows set in a deep wall and, in consequence, have seen only small sectors of the landscape outside. For these scholars and critics, certain meanings become very clear and irrefutable, even though they will often admit that other viewpoints are possibly valid. Critics with a less restricted view of the texts have argued against any dogmatism, claiming that Shakespeare held many opinions without proposing any one of them. For example, having examined the changes in Shakespeare's reputation down the centuries, Jonathan Bate came to believe that Shakespeare speaks particularly to the present sceptical age because he has 'proved himself peculiarly adaptable to a world of ambiguity, uncertainty, and relativity'.[6] He argued that Shakespeare's study of rhetoric when still a schoolboy had encouraged him to present both sides of any argument, so that his plays operate in a 'performative' manner, their many meanings discovered through enactment. In short, 'because he animated so many opposing voices, he has been able to speak to many later dispositions'.[7]

Theatre research has often gone along with this essentially literary approach to the plays, finding that records of performances from the earliest to present times provide evidence of an extraordinary diversity of interpretation. For example, a prolonged search among reviews, anecdotes, and biographies led Marvin Rosenberg to write of Shakespeare's 'polyphony', as if a number of different sounds or meanings could be heard interacting together in harmony.[8] Teachers of acting have also followed Shakespearean criticism and instructed actors to make 'choices' as if they were faced by a series of dilemmas that have multiple solutions that must be solved one way or other, leaving other possible interpretations to other occasions. Directors have followed the same lead in choosing a 'concept' or meaningful interpretation of a text that knowingly excludes other possible meanings and sets limitations to what may be discovered in rehearsal. In theatres, as in studies and classrooms, Shakespeare's art has been considered multivalent, full of opposing meanings and uncommitted to any one of them.

Theatrical study leads us to modify these views in two significant ways. First, performance of a Shakespeare play seldom articulates any meaning in words alone: those are likely to be supplied by members of an audience after the event, or by readers of a text with time to reflect and reconsider without experiencing the play coming to life before them. In theatrical performance, physical presence and not speech makes the greatest impression on an audience and this will vary according to the idiosyncratic nature of each actor. Moreover the most potent effects of performance are felt rather than understood: they are received by the senses and never wholly dependent on an intellectual recognition that can be verbalized.[9] The arousal of pleasure, fear, horror, anger, desire, affection, peace, devotion are among a play's most powerful functions and only if criticism takes into account the sensations belonging to these feelings and seeks out their causes can it hope to evaluate a play's processes and achievements. The dance of theatre – actors performing on stage with their whole beings, over a period of time – is the element for which the plays were written, not the speaking of their texts or the dissemination of any verbalized meaning or argument.

Secondly, and nevertheless, the end effect of a performance is seldom ambiguous, uncertain, or fragmentary. The experience of an audience is progressive: as each moment is affected by those preceding it, its members are caught up in a response that develops and finally encompasses the whole play.[10] Unless the production is botched or the actors lack experience, the effect is cumulative and finally, perhaps, concerted – one that only subsequent thought can analyse and evaluate in words. This means that no moment in a play can be rightly assessed without considering the effect of preceding moments: no word or action exists alone but rather they are part of a process that contributes to a progressive experience that may grow 'to something of great constancy'.[11] Shakespearean meanings, in so far as that is an appropriate term, are not only 'performative' and the result of dialogue or debate; they are also experiential and the result of process and growth. If we look exclusively for issues, conflict, or argument, we will miss the organic and progressive aspects of theatrical experience, qualities that these plays share with our lives.

From these basic characteristics of Shakespeare's plays in performance derives a third: the more freely and imaginatively an audience member responds to the ongoing action, the more deeply involved he or she will become with the play and, consequently, with the text from which the entire experience has sprung. For each person, the performance is like a kite that is fastened to the line of the text and carried by the wind in many different directions, at various levels and with varying force: it would collapse and fall to the ground were it not for the line that is held by the author who stands on his own ground and cunningly manipulates flight.

Some critics have concluded that Shakespeare had an 'open mind' on all, or almost all, the topics handled in his plays. Yet we know with equal certainty that he was so possessed by a drive to experiment and push forward the scope of his art that he chose to deal repeatedly with current issues of all kinds. Moreover he was so skilful in expressing ideas strongly and provocatively that producers and directors have used his plays, with some modifications or additions, to advocate many partisan beliefs and specific social or judicial initiatives. Rather than think that Shakespeare was indifferent to the needs of the world in which he lived, we might envisage him as passionately concerned to open the ears and eyes of his audiences to all the realities of that world by repeatedly drawing an intense or questioning view of a play's action.

Shakespeare belonged to a company of actors who in a single week could play many parts and give themselves as willingly to one as to another, to Edmund or Edgar, Shylock or Antonio, Falstaff or King Henry the Fourth.

And this company had to give pleasure to audiences in London and the regions, to the many individuals who came to the theatre full of their own concerns which were the product of their various lives in different places and among different classes of society. It also had to work under the censorship of a court official who was empowered to forbid the treatment of current politics or matters of religion. Whatever Shakespeare might 'most powerfully and potently' have believed (*Hamlet*, II.ii.201–2), there were many reasons for not writing plays that clearly represented his personal beliefs. His way was to conjure and lead audiences and readers to let the play have its own way, while the imagination of each one of them re-creates what happens on stage to suit each occasion and to reflect their own lives.

Notes

1. See pp. 74–7, above.
2. See p. 42, above.
3. See Dennis Kennedy, *Looking at Shakespeare*, 2nd edition (Cambridge: Cambridge University Press, 2001), *passim*.
4. See, for example, John Russell Brown, *New Sites for Shakespeare: Theatre, the Audience and Asia* (London and New York: Routledge, 1999), especially Part I.
5. See, for example, John Russell Brown, *Shakespeare and the Theatrical Event* (Basingstoke: Palgrave Macmillan, 2002), pp. 53–60.
6. Jonathan Bate, *The Genius of Shakespeare* (London: Picador, 1997), p. 330.
7. *Ibid.*, p. 330.
8. Marvin Rosenberg, *The Masks of Macbeth* (Berkeley and Los Angeles: University of California Press, 1978), p. x and *passim*.
9. See, especially, Chapters 3 and 5, above.
10. See, especially, Chapter 2, above.
11. *A Midsummer Night's Dream*, V.i.26.

Index